The Betjeman Society
1988 – 2008

A Scrapbook
of the First Twenty Years

compiled by
Philippa Davies

and edited by
Michael Richardson

The Betjeman Society
2009

Copyright:
The authors, other contributors and copyright holders

Published in 2009 by
The Betjeman Society and Mickle Print (Canterbury) Limited.

All rights reserved. No parts of this publication may be reproduced, stored in a retrieval system or transmitted in any form or by any means without the prior permission of the copyright holders.

ISBN: 978-0-9559997-1-0

Cover Picture: *Westminster Abbey 2001* by Ptolemy Dean
Pen and watercolour highlighting Poets' Corner and the Cartouche dedicated to Sir John Betjeman

Typesetting and Printing by MICKLE PRINT (Canterbury) Limited
Simmonds Road, Wincheap Estate, Canterbury, Kent CT1 3RA
www.mickleprint.com

This scrapbook is dedicated to
Michael Richardson
With love and thanks

A gentle guest, a willing host,
Affection deeply planted –
It's strange that those we miss the most
Are those we take for granted.

From *The Hon Sec* by John Betjeman

BETJEMAN'S COUNTRY

Loud over LERWICK,
seabirds wail and squawk

FINDOCHTY
findon
finglas
finstere

I stand exultant, neutral, free,
Behold a huge consoling sea

Great Gibbs of ABERDEEN

SIR JOHN BETJEMAN was born in 1906 in London. His early years were spent in Highgate. After school at Marlborough in Wiltshire he went up to Magdalen College, Oxford, where he forged life-long friendships.

His father hoped his only child would take over the family firm whose fortune had been made patenting the Tantalus. However John had other ideas. As a boy he had written "I knew as soon as I could read and write that I must be a poet".

Briefly he became a teacher, then journalist, film critic and author. A popular presenter on television and wireless, he campaigned for endangered buildings, was a champion for the Church of England and an authority on architecture. Fame came with the publication of his Collected Poems in 1958 and in time he was knighted and created Poet Laureate.

Happy childhood holidays were spent in Trebetherick in North Cornwall. Later he bought a house and took his own family down there.

He died in 1984 and is buried in the churchyard of his beloved St Enodoc.

In Westminster Abbey there is a glorious stone cartouche to his memory in Poets Corner.

Think of what our Nation stands for,
Books from Boots and country lanes,
Free speech, free passes, class distinction,
Democracy and proper drains.

THE LAST LAUGH
I made hay while
the sun shone.
My work sold.
Now if the harvest
is over
And the world cold,
Give me the
bonus of laughter
As I lose hold.

Now all ye pension'd army men
from Tunbridge Wells to PERTH

EDINBURGH
'The Athens of the North'

The emblem of The Betjeman Society

the waves in commotion
are tumbling about round
the long point of AYR

Spirit of Grasmere
bells of Ambleside,
sing you and ring you,
water bells, for me.

Through the midlands of IRELAND, I journeyed by diesel

Archie

On MANNIN'S
rough coastline
the twilight descending

O, I wad gang tae HARROGATE

JOHN BETJEMAN
1906-1984
Poet laureate

ROSCOMMON, thin
in ash-tree shadows.

In the licorice fields of PONTEFRACT
My love and I did meet

Oh, gay lapped the waves
on the shores of Lough Ennel

The sweet susurration
of incoming sea.

Sound soft LANCASTRIAN airs

Kirkby with Muckby-cum-Sparrowby-cum-Spinx Is down a long lane in the county of LINCS

Lush KILDARE
of scented meadows

Snowdon rises
in pearl-grey air.

The small
towns of
IRELAND
by bords
are neglected

And the Angelus is calling
Through DUNGARVAN in the train.

The Works in BIRMINGHAM
I knew, made glass –

Dear Mary, yes it will be bliss
To go with you by train to DISS

From over
LEAMINGTON SPA

Edwardian
ESSEX
opens wide

Foams to the Malvern Hills,
like an inland sea,

OXFORD May mornings
when the prunus bloomed
In that cluster of villages
LONDON by name

Proud City of BATH
with your crescents and
squares

Miss J. Hunter Dunn,
Miss J. Hunter Dunn,
Furnish'd and burnish'd
by ALDERSHOT sun

Hark I hear
the bells of WESTGATE

Dear lanes of Cornwall! With a one-inch map,
A bicycle and well-worn Little Guide.

Come, friendly bombs,
and fall on SLOUGH

Straight lines of hops
in pale brown earth of KENT

Blessed be ST ENODOC, blessed be the wave,
Blessed be the springy turf, we pray, pray to thee –

the MARLBOROUGH terms
form into seasons –

Celebrating the Centenary
of the birth of Sir John Betjeman.

Philippa Davies fecit

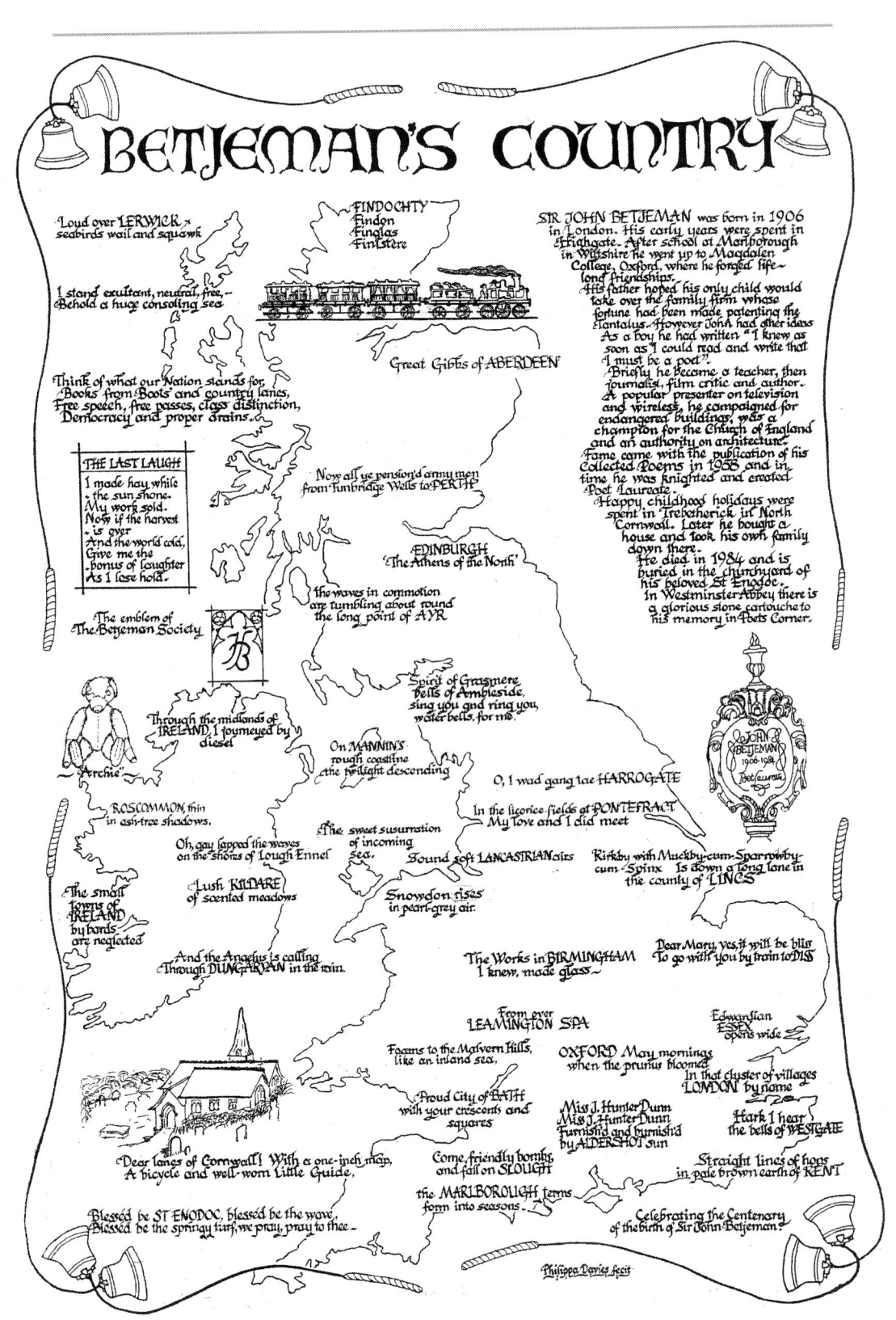

This poetical tour of The British Isles, through snatches of JB's verse, was created to celebrate the Centenary of his birth. With all Society news, this may be viewed on the Society website www.johnbetjeman.com .

iv   *A scrapbook of the first twenty years*

Acknowledgements

The idea of a Scrapbook began ten years ago as a collection of our history. After an energetic burst, the work languished. Whilst in suspense and after discussions and advice from those mentioned below, it became apparent that changes would improve the result.

Soon after our visit to Hull with the Larkin Society in 2005, Mike Richardson and I discussed the History of the Betjeman Society. The Lincolnshire Branch's publication *Betjeman's Lincolnshire*, edited by Mike, was on its way to publication and about to be launched to critical acclaim. Mike may have been buoyed by its success or missed the buzz of writing and deadlines but with that under his belt he told me in a weak moment he could do with a little occupational therapy. In the end, the task turned out to be far from little. How glad I am that he offered his help and was declared Editor.

In order for Mike to proceed, we were given the blessing of John Heald, as Chairman, and members of the Council. David Pattison, our current Chairman, has continued with support for the book. Peter Gammond always kept the project simmering and assured me it would happen. Martin Revill unhesitatingly kept himself available to assist. Bevis Hillier guided the opening paragraphs, offered a few improvements and tactfully suggested deletions, none more important than the dreadful overuse of exclamation marks or, in his words, gaspers. Horace Liberty squeezes more into a day than anyone I know, and when asked for help sent his copy almost by return of post. Early on Ken Pinnock had wise advice about the structure of a preface. Professor Mike Irwin and Dr Peter Brown from the School of English at the University of Kent kindly read the first drafts and made suggestions that we have gratefully accepted and absorbed. My husband, Jake, has understood when I needed peace and frequently acted as a sounding board or lent a sympathetic ear.

Mike Richardson's calm and gentlemanly way made every letter and phone call a pleasure to receive, and every visit to Mike and Ellen's beautiful house a delight. From his home in Tennyson country in Lincolnshire twixt Old Bolingbroke and Mavis Enderby has come, not the "gift of a son" as some local wit was once seen to have pinned to the signpost, but another publication of which the Betjeman Society can be proud. Place names such as these amused JB and this story is told in Volume 2 of Bevis's masterly biography, *New Fame, New Love*. Mike told me in the autumn that he was having problems with his health and could spend only limited hours working at his computer. This could have spelt the end of the Scrapbook but for Margaret Revill who so gently and generously offered her secretarial skills to help to finish the book and saved the day – pure serendipity.

Everybody who was invited to write has done so eagerly and these original words and articles add to the interest. A few of our members have dispersed and some have died* since sending their contributions and this has made their pieces even more valued. Mickle Print have been very helpful and I believe Tim Ashenden is as pleased with the result of their work as we are.

This is my opportunity to put on record my gratitude. I wish to thank all those named and un-named who have prepared and read our publications, come to our events, shared in our fun and everyone who ever was and is a member of the Betjeman Society.

Philippa Davies

Philippa Davies
Haleswood
January 2009

Since these acknowledgements were written we have been greatly saddened by the untimely death of Michael Richardson who played such a major part in the compilation of this book. I should like to add his name to the top of my list of thanks and dedicate the Scrapbook to his memory.

Signpost near Spilsby, Lincolnshire

CONTENTS

	page
Title page, verso	i, ii
Acknowledgements	iii
Contents	vii

Preface — 1

History
- Origins of the Society — 3
- Constitution — 10
- Organisation — 12
- Membership History — 15
- Printing and design — 18
- Publications — 21
- Bibliographical companion — 27

People
- Presidents and Vice-Presidents — 29
- John (Jock) Murray — 30
- Lord (Mervyn) Horder — 32
- Lady (Mary) Wilson — 33

Questionnaire to President and Vice-Presidents — 35
Officers of the Society — 45

Branches History — 47
- 1989 Sherborne — 49
- 1990 Canterbury — 51
- 1995 Wantage — 53
- 1996 Oxford (refounded 2006) — 58
- 1997 The Shires — 59
- 1999 Isle of Man — 62
- 1999 Lincolnshire — 64
- 2008 Ridings — 66

Bygone Branches   66
    1989-1997 Bristol/Weston-Super-Mare
    1990-1995 Oxford University
    1991-1998 Birmingham
    1994-1999 Ireland

Events   69
Red Letter Days
    1990   Marlborough   69
    1998   Westminster Abbey   71
    2006   Centenary of JB's birthday   73
    2007   JB at St Pancras   77

Diary: 1987 to 2008   80

Epilogue   93

Appendices
    Synopsis of life of Sir John Betjeman   95
    A brief Betjeman Bibliography   99
    List of Subscribers   101

PREFACE

Philippa Davies

Some years ago I went to Highgate Cemetery to investigate the possibility of a visit for the Society. I knocked on the door of the office and a formidable lady firmly informed me "I am sorry, we are closed." .... "Oh what a pity, I had hoped to enquire about The Betjeman Society booking a tour." .... "Oh, John Betjeman, do come in."

This story is one of many when doors have been opened merely by the mention of his name. Not only has Betjeman opened doors, he has also opened our eyes, ears and minds to unexpected glories. Through his poems and prose we have been encouraged to look up at roofs, eaves, spires, windows, churches galore and railway stations of cathedral proportions. We have looked at medieval and encaustic tiles, cast-iron street furniture and coal holes, even poems set into the floor at St Pancras Station. In the name and cause of Betjeman we have had opportunities to appreciate our heritage, both built and written, with an enquiring and fresh approach.

Our first gathering of a room full of friends simply enjoying a few poems hardly heralded a national society. Never could we have conceived that one day we would have members or rub shoulders with experts in many fields. We never imagined a Society that would grow into a worldwide resource and produce notable publications such as *A Bibliographical Companion to Betjeman*, its follow-up *A Betjeman Checklist* and *Betjeman's Lincolnshire*. Our mix of members and Branches all fit in somewhere between broad and wide. Their interests and membership of other groups are dazzling.

The personality of Betjeman must be responsible for this mix. We name but a few of these wider societies and interests: Thomas Hardy, Anthony Powell, Dymock poets, John Clare, Philip Larkin, City liverymen, the Victorian Society, railway enthusiasts, churches high and low, Round Church Tower Society, campanologists, Prayer Book Society, Green Line buses, Wimbledon linesmen, Music Hall songs, British peers and British piers.

There have been many high points. One of the first must be meeting the Murray family. Jock became Betjeman's publisher and, like him, was also an Oxford and Magdalen man. Jock and Diana Murray so kindly invited the fledgling group to meet them at Murray's publishing house, 50 Albemarle Street. Jock had no idea who we were but with gusto he flew into the famous drawing room and welcomed us warmly. With absolute trust and generosity they laid out precious archives and drowned us in freely flowing wine. Through him we made contact with Bevis Hillier and Ken Pinnock. Volume 1 of Bevis Hillier's biography of Betjeman had been published but we were able to share in Bevis's joy with the publication of Volumes 2 and 3.

Probably our most exciting moment was the occasion of the dedication of the cartouche to Sir John Betjeman in Poets' Corner in Westminster Abbey. There were many discussions about the principle and later about the position for a memorial. Dean Mayne explained it was an unwritten rule that to be considered one had to have been dead for at least ten years. However, he was in no doubt that there was sufficiently strong and lasting interest for Betjeman to be a contender for a coveted place. As for position, the first place mentioned was for a memorial stone on an area of floor in a central area of Poets' Corner. Later there was an idea of a memorial occupying one of a series of glass panels on a high east window of the south transept. Finally, an 18th century cartouche was found in the lapidarium. Once this had the approval of Jock Murray and Betjeman's daughter, Candida Lycett Green, Donald Buttress and David Peace were invited to design the lettering and embellishments. There it rests today in all its glory at eye level on one of the pillars.

There have been low points too. Our first secretary, Vicky Phillips, managed the membership so well but after she left we had problems. We also had difficulties with listing the Society's archive. Now it is in safe keeping in Highgate Literary and Scientific Institute. On one occasion there was a meeting when we were due to be shown City of London churches. With an ominous absence of our leader and with a full list of members at the gates of Bart's we heard the sad news that the church expert, Lawrence Jones, had just died. One of our members, Tim Heath, rescued the day and read poetry in the crypt of St Paul's.

Hardly a week goes by without a mention of Betjeman in the press or on the wireless. The word Betjemanesque is entering dictionaries and common parlance. Nevertheless we still need to spread the word and worth of the Society far and wide, win more publicity and particularly enrol young people. It was most encouraging to visit Giggleswick school recently. The head of English there told me they love Betjeman and have recitals. More, more we say! Troupes of travelling players who are members and friends of the Betjeman Society entertain and raise money for charities and good causes. The Sherborne Branch, The Gammond and Heald Trio, Keith Hutton and Richard Morley and their group, Lance Pierson who appeared at the Edinburgh Festival, and the Betjeman Players introduce new audiences to poetry and prose.

The World Wide Web has enormous potential and electronic communication and email must be the way forward. Perhaps we shall soon use chat rooms, blogs and message boards. These were rarely thought of 20 years ago but who can guess how this and other societies will be managed ten years hence? Can anyone know for how much longer we shall have whistling milkmen or postmen on bicycles?

The purpose of this Scrapbook is to look back, but also to look forward. All whom we have encountered on our journey of 20 years have made the Society what it is and everything it stands for. Some members join just to receive our Newsletters and annual journal. Others support meetings and outings. Every member is equal and special.

Flick through these pages at leisure and stop where you will. Enjoy the stories and pictures. Use the ready reference diary for dates and locations of every Society event. Read about our Presidents and Vice-Presidents. Enjoy members' memories and indulge in passages from our Betjemanians and Newsletters. Whatever changes we may next experience, we hope we will all continue to enjoy the friendship of The Betjeman Society.

ORIGINS OF THE BETJEMAN SOCIETY

Philippa Davies

Beside the oak stair

My childhood was sheltered and utterly happy. Tennis, golf, tobogganing on the golf course and parties, parties, parties filled my holidays. I lived and played in a very restricted world. The school my parents sent me to was called Farringtons. It was a Methodist girls' school in the comfortable commuter belt of Kent, in leafy Chislehurst. Every day at 1.15 we had lunch and then, bliss, we had games all afternoon until tea then more classes. As a so-called day-boarder I went home at 6.40 with my prep. Weekends had the added excitement for those who were in teams to play in matches. Of the schools on our fixture list, Benenden was a favourite. We often played against girls we knew well and whom we met in the holidays at teenage dances. Did we win or lose those matches? I really can't remember. I know we all played our hearts out in the most sporting way.

It was around that time in 1959 when I was struggling with English and "difficult" poetry at school, that my mother gave me a little book of verse by John Betjeman in Hulton's collection of Pocket Poets. It was a revelation. This was different from anything I had read before. It rhymed and I could understand it. It must be poetry, it said so on the cover. Later my mother gave me a copy of *Collected Poems*, which had recently been published in paperback, to wish me luck in my A levels. But it was that slim volume that opened my eyes to the rhythm of words and the

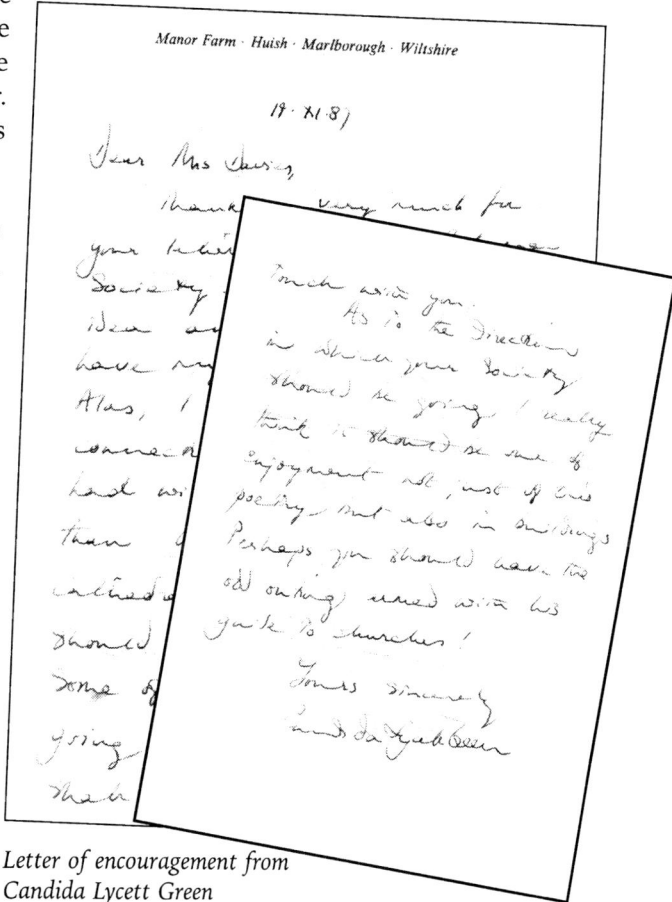

Letter of encouragement from Candida Lycett Green

built and natural world around me, and that really paved the way to the formation of our Society. The poems were about subjects I knew and enjoyed such as dances, golf, tennis tournaments, the Home Counties and so on. *Seaside Golf* and *A Subaltern's Love Song* sent me reeling with joy. John Betjeman's words were engraved on my heart and gave me such comfort in times of joy or trouble. Who was this man with a funny name, who spoke to me, I wondered?

On the occasions of away matches at Benenden our hostesses escorted us into the very grand main house and up to the dormitories to change; then we came down for an enormous and welcome tea. What I remember was standing on the top stair, pausing and looking down imagining it was exactly like the staircase in *A Subaltern's Love Song*, with pictures, possibly of Egypt, bright on the wall. But I knew that I, in days before contact lenses, wearing glasses with lenses like bottle bottoms and even curlier hair from hurtling around the tennis court or lacrosse pitch, could never dream that a dinner-jacketed beau would be waiting in the hall for me.

I did dream of meeting the poet but I honestly didn't know one could meet such people. I knew composers of music were dead because all those we heard about at school had lived long ago. I somehow knew Betjeman was alive but wouldn't have known how on earth to make contact. Had I done, what would I have said? It was this hesitation and ignorance that led more directly to the founding of the Society. Even though the story was told in the first Journal, it is worth repeating and I am sinfully proud to confess to an act of imposture.

The act of imposture
This is the story of how the deception came about. One day, some weeks after JB died, the expected notice appeared in the press. A Memorial Service was to be held at Westminster Abbey on St Peter's Day, 29th June 1984. I may not have had the pluck to meet the great man in life but I felt so upset at his death and such disappointment at not having met him that I was determined to get to this service. I decided I would write a letter immediately asking for tickets.

There were "postal difficulties" at the time but those should prove no obstacle. Somehow I would travel to London and deliver the letter by hand to Dean's Yard. I could easily write saying how long and how much I admired our late Poet Laureate. But what if hundreds of fans were to write in the same vein? We would never fit into the Abbey. I screwed up my first letter, paused, and let my pen decide what to write. The words that appeared looked far more likely to succeed. There I was, styled as "the representative of The Canterbury Betjeman Society". How could I style myself thus? But write it I did. Deliver it I did. And lucky I was. I asked for two tickets and I invited Sarah Taylor to join me. I had met Sarah ten years previously when I was in hospital, pregnant with our third child. Although we were more or less chained to our beds for a few weeks in the antenatal ward and I was drugged to stop me talking, Sarah and I knew that despite being at the furthest corners of the ward we were soul mates. Sarah was a teacher of English and Drama, I had an amateur love of words and all our children were of similar ages.

HISTORY: *Origins of the Society*

Because of the postal problems, there was no way I could receive any sort of confirmation of tickets until the day but I must have felt confident enough to take a day away from my work and encourage my friend to join me in my mission.

Lo and behold! Two brown tickets in an envelope bearing my name awaited us in the small marquee at the entrance to the Abbey. Sarah and I made our way slowly down the nave to a most privileged position in Poets' Corner, no less. I had never been to a Memorial Service before and this was of such importance and scale. The emotions that I felt were of excitement, pride and shame all rolled into one. I whispered to Sarah "Don't speak to anyone. They might ask us what we do". Knowing nothing of literary societies or even if there was an established Betjeman Society in Canterbury, there was a danger we might be rumbled. The saying that "all beginnings are delightful, the threshold is the place to pause" could not have been more apposite than for that occasion. We paused and pinched ourselves many times. The service was quite amazing. The entire choir and congregation and it seemed every stone of the Abbey itself enjoyed it all to the full. My gratitude for those tickets was overwhelming.

Inhibited by shame we slipped silently away anonymously through a little back door into the sunshine and the Abbey precincts. That, I thought, is that. It could have been that. With the mission complete, there was no one to thank, no one to be told.

Initially my instinct was to lie low after that marvellous Memorial Service and to do nothing. However, guilt gradually overwhelmed me and, nearly three years later, with new-found courage I felt bound to honour my claim to be the representative of The Canterbury Betjeman Society.

WESTMINSTER ABBEY

SERVICE OF THANKSGIVING
for the Life and Work of
SIR JOHN BETJEMAN
CBE

1906—1984

POET LAUREATE

St Peter's Day
Friday 29 June 1984
11.30 a.m.

A scrapbook of the first twenty years

HISTORY: *Origins of the Society*

People I knew convinced me that even Betjeman would have been amused by the fraud. All that was needed was to find enough fellow lovers of his work who would like to spend just one evening sharing favourite poems.

The great storm of October 1987 was about to flatten many of the woods of southeast England: otherwise all was going well in my world. Our children were at school and heading for university, I had resumed my practice of physiotherapy, I played tennis and went for walks, joined evening classes and looked after home and family but I hadn't much spare time.

On an October evening that year I invited a gathering of friends to my home. We read a wide selection of Betjeman's poetry. It was the most self-indulgent evening that I can remember. Our next soiree was held a few months later in the spring of 1988 and it was there that I broke the news that we were the one and only Betjeman Society. As the perpetrator of the fraud three years earlier, it morally fell to me to decide the next move. At that stage we could not have known what lay round the corner. Responsibilities were about to begin. It was suggested that we make contact with other Societies which were also lovers of Betjeman. There was no doubt in my mind that they must exist and be scattered throughout the country. Just how could we find them? Write to his publisher! Who was he?

There really was a John Murray and I was utterly unprepared for his reply, friendly and helpful. "What a delightful idea – which I would support in any way I can". But there were, it seemed, no other similar groups. Would I write to Betjeman's daughter and his principal literary executor? It dawned on me that we were being catapulted overnight from a little Canterbury group to the one and only worldwide Betjeman Society. Candida Lycett Green and Lady Elizabeth Cavendish could have had no idea how much pleasure their letters would give and how their encouragement unleashed our energy. Candida wrote: "I am sure it would have my father's approval. I think [the Society] should be one of enjoyment not just of his poetry but also buildings. Perhaps you should have the odd outing armed with his guide to churches!" Lady Elizabeth suggested, "You should go on from reading his poetry to enjoy Tennyson, Cowper and Wordsworth who were his favourites".

So far, so good. What next? Could I or anyone else have had any idea how much computers, email, piles of paper, book collecting, letter writing, committees, new friends and an enormous wealth of meetings and events would envelop me and everyone else who would serve on the council and committees of the Betjeman Society?

The Society's inaugural meeting

I turned to my friend, Edred Wright, who had just retired from his job as Director of Music at The King's School, Canterbury. All praise to him for never telling me how to proceed or taking over the development of ideas. He calmly asked me what did I think we should do? I thought we should have a public meeting. What do we need for that? Well we need a venue and we need to be able to issue tickets and we certainly need publicity and to find an attractive speaker. Edred knew Mike Irwin, Professor of English

Literature at the University of Kent. He agreed to phone Mike then and there. Mike readily accepted our invitation to speak, all just for a bottle of wine. We had a date and an eye-catching title. Through another of my friends, Vicky Phillips, we were offered a smart room for the meeting called the Societies Room at The King's School. The Tourist Information Office in Canterbury agreed to give out tickets. As for publicity, the editor of the *Kentish Gazette*, Alan Bensted, helped. He had met me through short physiotherapy articles I had written for our local paper. He was excited by the idea of the Society and not only agreed to print copy I gave him but suggested sending a photographer; "one picture is worth a thousand words etc".

The whole idea caught the eye of so many people. Issuing tickets, albeit free ones, indicated that with greater numbers than expected, we needed to make a hasty change of venue. The first public meeting of The Betjeman Society was thus held in the larger Egyptian style Old Synagogue, another property of the King's School. The evening was very snowy. Such unseasonable weather could put faint-hearted people right off and the thought of an evening by the fire could have seemed more tempting. Never mind the weather, people came in droves. We knew rough numbers from ticket issues but others arrived hoping not to be turned away. Loyal friends, learned locals and all interested parties were warmly welcomed. We had a full house.

Mike Irwin chose the title *Toothbrush, Tram and Tennis Racket*. It must have been a good lecture, judging by the applause and questions. The only part I remember was his description of Parliament Hill Fields where he and JB had both lived and been educated. I have asked him since whether he could recall his text. He had no memory of it nor had he kept lecture notes. Having never presided over such a meeting I declare I was ill-prepared and surprised by the size of the audience. We did pass a list round and some signed it and we passed a hat around and took a small collection. Throughout the meeting I was racking my brain, wondering what to do next.

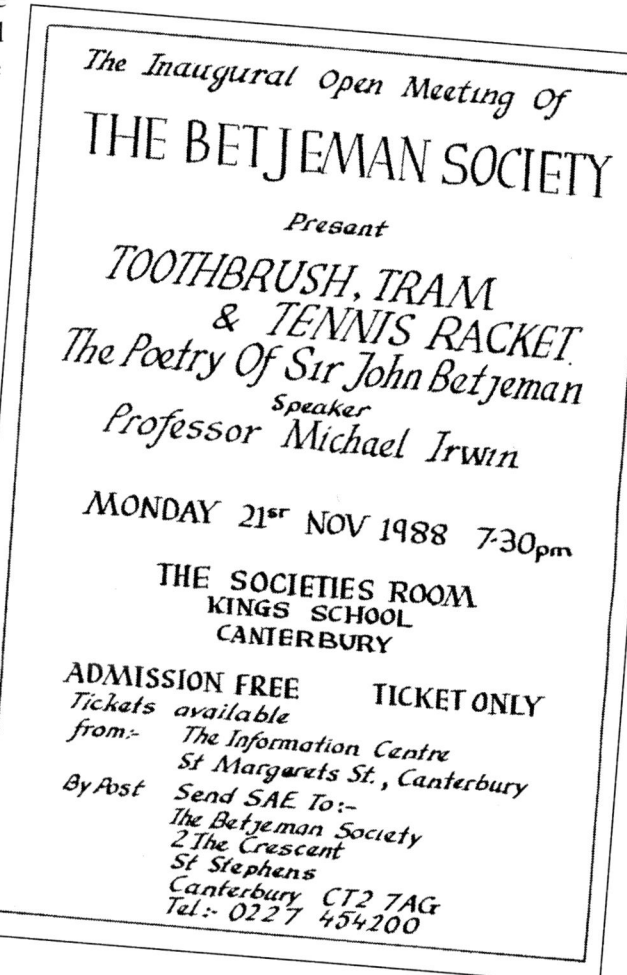

> The Inaugural Open Meeting Of
> **THE BETJEMAN SOCIETY**
> Present
> *TOOTHBRUSH, TRAM & TENNIS RACKET*
> The Poetry Of Sir John Betjeman
> Speaker
> Professor Michael Irwin
> MONDAY 21ˢᵗ NOV 1988 7·30pm
> THE SOCIETIES ROOM
> KINGS SCHOOL
> CANTERBURY
> ADMISSION FREE   TICKET ONLY
> Tickets available
> from :- The Information Centre
>   St Margarets St., Canterbury
> By Post Send SAE To :-
>   The Betjeman Society
>   2 The Crescent
>   St Stephens
>   Canterbury CT2 7AG
>   Tel :- 0227 454200

HISTORY: *Origins of the Society*

After the lecture

Obviously the audience was enthusiastic and I realised I had to strike while the iron was hot. It was a Monday evening so presumably this crowd was not otherwise committed on that night of the week. I enquired whether they would like another meeting and as they most certainly would I invited people to come forward to help me plan one. There we were, eight volunteers, at our house one week later. Jim Gibson, a Thomas Hardy specialist and one-time Chairman of the Hardy Society, who had been told by Helen, his wife, to enjoy the meeting but NOT to get involved, Edred Wright, who was always there when needed, Vicky Phillips who was encouraged by her husband, the Headmaster of King's School, Helen Warner, Ian Ward, John Lissaman, an accountant and host of our second house group meeting, and my husband, Jake, also an accountant, who couldn't escape.

We justifiably discussed the success of our first public meeting but had to decide what to do next. When I went out to the kitchen to make coffee the obvious move struck me. Form a committee. Everyone should be offered a job they could cope with and thankfully they all agreed. Jim was ideal for Chairman, Edred for Vice, Jake for Hon Treasurer - a small job to care for the £17+ collected the previous week. Vicky was Membership Secretary but with no members; John offered to be auditor should he be needed and Helen and Ian were general committee members. I decided I should take on the role of Hon Secretary in case there ever was a heavy workload.

The next dilemma was how to get in touch with other Betjeman fans and let the world at large know that there was a Betjeman Society. Initially we knew we must design and pay for stationery. Thanks to Jim and Helen's experience, and the confidence we must have felt to underwrite the costs, we set off to Thanet Printing Works. The design of our first logo by Ray Evison is told in another section. The design of the membership form took time. As each hurdle was overcome we thought we were there.

To find members or just to tell people about the Society we needed national publicity and Jim wrote a press release. *The Times, Daily Telegraph* and *Independent* printed snatches of his offering and although they were poked into hidden corners of these papers they were spotted by many readers. The hundreds of replies and telephone calls that followed almost overwhelmed us. *The Independent* called me Mrs Haleswood, the name of our house which, although a typographical error, was a useful lesson for sourcing. We had membership forms to send out, headed writing paper to reply on and money coming in. It was such an exciting time. We needed very frequent committee meetings and renamed ourselves the Council. We arranged meetings, initially in Canterbury, and gradually further afield. Looking back it is easy to see the Society was gradually developing its future pattern.

For our first meeting away from Canterbury, the owners of the then recently opened Wine Bar in Betjeman's former home, 43 Cloth Fair, Smithfield, invited us to the unveiling of the Blue Plaque there and on that same evening we held our first London dinner at Betjeman's Wine Bar.

HISTORY: *Origins of the Society*

Mrs Doris Lurot Betjeman and Pennie Denton at Betjeman's Wine Bar Dinner.

First London Dinner, Betjeman's Wine Bar, 43 Cloth Fair, June 1989

Of the thirty people present then, several joined the Council and over half came to our second London dinner ten years later. At that first dinner we met a cousin and an aunt of Betjeman. We also met Robert Shaw, an architect who, as an old boy, would be our link with Marlborough College for the Joan Hunter Dunn tennis tournament, and who also started the Newsletter as we now know it.

We had a picnic at St Enodoc, and we met Bevis Hillier in Hampstead. Both of these meetings had good press publicity. We sponsored an event in the Canterbury Festival, held a tea dance at the Waldorf and attracted more publicity in *The Mail*. We invited Pennie Denton to speak to the Society at the Poetry Library in the Royal Festival Hall and we held more meetings in Canterbury. We welcomed the Betjeman group in Sherborne, formed our branch in Canterbury, and Ken Pinnock drew up an advertiser's card. Mention in the press through our Vice-Presidents, Auberon Waugh, Candida Lycett Green and various other sources was hugely beneficial. Despite anticipation of electronic life, the written word and meetings of minds and friends still appeal most to the majority of our membership.

A scrapbook of the first twenty years

THE CONSTITUTION

Jake Davies

The first attempts at drafting a constitution had two main purposes, simplicity and charitable status. Examples were studied from a variety of sources, the most influential of which was the National Council of Voluntary Organisations (NCVO). The NCVO provided a "Specimen constitution for an unincorporated organisation having a membership (seeking charitable status)."

The Society was fortunate in benefiting from the services of Kenneth Poole, who was a neighbour and friend of Edred Wright. Kenneth worked at the University of Kent and possessed considerable legal and drafting skills. Within weeks he distilled from these various documents a draft constitution. It is no small credit to his work that this has survived various reviews by the Charity Commissioners and others with only minor amendments.

*Shaping the Constitution in 1989
left to right: Robert Shaw, Ken Poole, Jake Davies, Jim Gibson*

The constitution as drafted by Kenneth Poole was, subject to three amendments, approved by the Charity Commissioners on 24 May 1990. The Commissioners also confirmed that the Inland Revenue had given their approval on 9 April 1990. It was subsequently approved at a Council Meeting held on 8 July 1990 and it was agreed that it should be put to the AGM held on 11 May 1991 for ratification. At that AGM it was decided that no further action should be taken towards the application for charitable status. A resolution to otherwise adopt the constitution should have been proposed but was deferred until later.

Four years on, at the AGM held in June 1995, it was announced that John Heald, Kenneth Pinnock and Brian Turner were studying the constitution with a view to recommending certain changes to the Council and, through that body, to the Society at large. The aim was to increase efficiency, reduce bureaucracy and remove a number of anomalies in existing practices. This task proved, however, to be more complicated than was originally envisaged and at the AGM in 1996 it was stated that progress was being made sorting out the constitution and that further information would be given in a forthcoming Newsletter.

A particular problem was the relationship, financial and otherwise, between the Branches and the Society. By the next AGM, on 21 June 1997, a new constitution had been drafted and made available to all members. It was adopted after minor amendment. Relationships with the Branches, however, had still not been adequately resolved.

On 10 June 2000, Clause 6 of the constitution was amended in the hope that the number of local Branches would increase and their influence would become stronger. An additional benefit to those Branch members who were also members of the Society was that they would be covered by the Society's insurances. Whilst even a small minority of non-members in the Branches may be considered undesirable, these do nevertheless represent potential future members. An analysis prepared in 2007 indicated that about 45 Branch members were not yet members of the Society. Further emphasis needs to be placed on the advantages of membership of the Society. A draft 'Branch Constitution' is currently being prepared for consultation and adoption as appropriate.

HOW WE GET ON IN THE SOCIETY

John Heald

Many years ago I received a telephone call from someone in the West Country who had been given my number by his local library. He understood I was involved in a society devoted to 'that chap Betjeman'. What was our purpose? What exactly did we do? And why? I did my best to satisfy him and this took me so long I was glad he was paying for the call. He thanked me. Two weeks later a new member had joined us and he has proved to be an active one.

The call, however, did give me something to think about. The Betjeman Society had been part of my life for many years: for most of them what seemed to be a full-time activity with, I must admit, generous time off for eating, drinking and sleeping - and the occasional evening out with my wife. I enjoyed the part I played but had never thought a lot about our function and was somewhat surprised that a librarian in Devon knew we existed at all.

In the end, I decided we were all manner of things. Our membership form says, quite rightly, that our aim is to promote the study and appreciation of Betjeman's life and work. But, surely, we are more than that. We are also a fan club, proud that Sir John has a place in the Poetic Premier League. Unlike The Philip Larkin Society, we have not yet produced a T-shirt (decorated by two lines from a poem concerning one's mum and dad) but we do have a splendid tie.

We are a study centre, forever learning more about a most remarkable and complicated man. We are an information desk answering questions of all kinds from newspapers, radio stations and from the public at large - very large, I sometimes think. My favourite was a request for me to identify the exact spot on the A30 where, in Sir John's meditation on road rage, 'the corner accepted its kill'. We are a think-tank, determining how we can best ensure that Betjeman's ideas, priorities and writing are neither misrepresented nor forgotten. We are a pressure group constantly reminding publishers, editors, broadcasters and others with influence that Betjeman is a name to be reckoned with. Finally, we are a society of friends who came together because of a shared interest and are staying together because we like one another.

I often think of that day in 1984 when my wife and I attended Westminster Abbey for Sir John's Memorial Service. We were shown to our seats by John Sparrow and tears were not far away as we realised where we were, part of a mighty throng there to honour and remember a great man. I was sitting next to the actor representing the cast and producers of 'Coronation Street' and, at the end of the service, we smiled, as Sir John would have wanted us to do, as the music of Jim Parker reminded us that the bonus of laughter will never be taken away.

Little did I know then that somewhere in the Abbey sat Philippa Davies with the thought of a Betjeman Society already in her mind. Margaret Thatcher infamously pronounced that there was no such thing as society. Philippa, a lady much more to my liking, knew better and, in fact, she created one!

As I write these words in May 2008, I am Chairman and a long-serving Council member. I was Vice-Chairman for some time and the Hon. Secretary for almost a decade and so I do know something about the running of the Society. The fact that it seems to run itself must never allow us to forget or underestimate the huge amount of activity taking place beneath the surface and often, literally, behind closed doors. Like all healthy bodies, we have a fine constitution and this document is the ultimate authority behind all we do and, indeed, behind our very existence. Great care was taken in the preparation of the first draft as Philippa and Jake Davies, Kenneth Pinnock and Edred Wright wanted to ensure that jargon and what is worse, legal jargon, was avoided at all costs. With the help of Ken Poole, from the University of Kent, a slim and simple document was produced. This satisfied the Charities Commission so that, if considered advisable, charitable status could be adopted.

Some time later Kenneth Pinnock, Brian Turner and I were asked to say whether, in the light of experience, any changes were desirable and the proposals we made then were fully approved by the membership.

As provided by the Constitution, a Council is elected each year and this consists of a Chairman, Vice-Chairman, Secretary, Treasurer and up to six other members. These are the people who deserve both thanks and support for, as I can confirm from my own experience, they work hard and perform many tasks - menial, onerous, time-consuming, exciting but all important and, in the end, worthwhile.

Council is entrusted with the job of keeping the Betjeman flag in the air, organising events, being effective public relations officers for Sir John and all he represents, coming up with good ideas and providing value for money. The Betjemanian, now edited by Horace Liberty who succeeded Peter Gammond two years ago, is regarded as a model journal of a literary society and I was recently told that it alone was worth the membership fee. He was right! Our regular Newsletter, beautifully and lovingly edited by John Cottenden and then by Michael Thomas, whose deaths have caused immense grief, is incredibly successful in imparting news, gossip and letting us keep in touch with one another.

Meetings of Council take place about six times each year and an extra meeting is usually arranged near the date of the AGM, that annual review of performance and future plans. There is no fixed venue for these meetings - we have met in private rooms in pubs and clubs, the impressive offices of the publisher John Murray and in our own homes but these days we tend to find the Union Jack Club convenient as it is a quiet oasis in a busy part of London and is also handy for Waterloo Station.

The minutes of these meetings record some furious debates, some friendly disputes and much enjoyable argument. They certainly prove that we all take the job seriously and try to be fair. We encourage and help the branches and are delighted they each have an individual identity - the happy exuberance of The Shires and the quiet fundraising of Sherborne, for example. It has now become the tradition for us to ask one of the branches to host the AGM every other year and this has produced some memorable days together. Who will ever forget morning coffee at the Deanery in Canterbury - with the Dean as our host? Or visits to Ardington House and Market Harborough?

Elsewhere in this book you will find information about our President and Vice-Presidents and about the help Council and the Society as a whole receives from them. I do not want to end my own contribution, however, without saying how fortunate we have been in our choice of 'friends in high places'. I never knew Jock Murray, the first President - or Patron as we then called him - but working with his three successors has been a sheer pleasure. If you want to know what makes a good President just think of Mervyn Horder, Mary Wilson and Bevis Hillier.

Those names say it all. Except thank you, to them and to all those who do so much to make sure that The Betjeman Society is not only useful but also jolly good fun.

John and Ann Heald buying tickets at Southend Pier to go on the Sir John Betjeman train, 1999.

MEMBERSHIP HISTORY

As a result of our 'press release' and first open meeting in Canterbury in 1988, we had over 200 members of the Society by the end of the following year, and by the end of 1993 there were 310 members. Numbers peaked in 2003 at 964 but, since then, they have fallen to 800.

Membership Secretaries:
>Vicky Phillips 1988-93
>James Luly 1993-94
>Gayne Wells 1994-2003
>Martin Revill 2003 to date

Vicky Phillips, wife of the Master of King's School, Canterbury, was our first Membership Secretary and she served on the Council from 1988 until her husband's work changed and they moved from Canterbury. She wrote in 1993:

>The Society has come a long way since that evening in October 1987 when Philippa and Jake Davies gathered about ten of their friends to read poems by Betjeman. A second meeting was held to which I went little knowing that an actual Society was to be formed. Before long I was approached and asked whether I would be Membership Secretary. It was a strong person who could resist Philippa's powers of persuasion and enthusiasm. It was an exciting time.

>Interest in the Society was shown right from the start and very soon enquiries were coming in from all over the country - and indeed abroad. Where had these people heard of us? Mostly I think it was a press release in a newspaper and word of mouth. After open meetings there were always requests for more information.

>My Betjeman Corner consisted of a couple of shoe boxes and a wadge of record cards which mushroomed to over 200 registered members in the first year. Oh! for a computer to deal with those alphabetical lists which had to be typed and retyped!

>I used to walk regularly over to Jake's (Hon Treasurer's) office to hand over and get queries sorted out. So easy when Membership Secretary, Treasurer and Chairman lived near one another. As always there was the occasional awkward would-be member.

>The Society was evolving fast and very soon we discovered there was another group which also met to discuss Betjeman in Sherborne. For our mutual enrichment this was eventually incorporated into our own Society and became the first Branch.

HISTORY: Membership

Those early days of the Society were very special with all the freshness and uncertainty of what the future held. With the Society continuing to attract new members, it is good to know that the future is assured.

After Vicky Phillips, **James Luly** held the post for less than two years but left suddenly, and a promise he had made when he took on the job, that he would bring us towards computerisation, was still unfulfilled. He was followed by **Gayne Wells** who was already a Council member and in his calm, modest and humorous way he got us out of a spot of bother. When he took the job on in 1994, the Society's membership records were unsatisfactory. Gayne remembers:

> When I received the membership list, my name was not there, despite having joined at Penny Denton's lecture at the Festival Hall in February 1990. Had it not been for reciprocal mailing with the London Society I would, no doubt, have forgotten all about the Betjeman Society.
>
> The membership stood at just over 300 and I was able to establish a card index system and follow up numerous enquiries and renewals. I also assumed responsibility for mailing, and data was loaded onto a computer so those labels could be amended and produced easily. The task of keeping the "shop" also came my way and this has expanded to reach 17 items of merchandise available for members to purchase.
>
> It has been an enjoyable role to play, in that success or failure is in one's own hands save, of course, for those essential new applications and renewals. There has been a steady increase in membership and thus of the resources of the Society during my stewardship.
>
> As with any organisation that opens its doors to the "world and his wife" one comes across some characters. A perennial problem is that between 30 and 40 people do not renew each year and do not respond to requests for either payment or a note of resignation. One member, having received a request in December, reminders in February and April and a "final notice" in July wrote. " I have looked into the matter and find that I have not had time to open your letter of February!" Still no indication as to whether he intended to renew or not: he was deleted – in July!
>
> In the early years I telephoned people as a last resort; no longer, as the cost is not justified by results. Having traced a number, via a building society, I rang an address in Skipton:
>
> "Mr _ _ _ _ _ please".
>
> "He died last year" (obviously the widow).
>
> "I'm so sorry. I do apologise. We're the Betjeman Society. We haven't been told have we?"
>
> "No – we keep getting your stuff and not doing owt about it; can yer cross him off?"
>
> To any member, I can certainly recommend taking an active part in the running of the Society. Without exception the Betjemanians are delightful people. It is a popular maxim that "The more you put in the more you get out" and this is certainly true of the Betjeman Society.

Gayne Wells was succeeded by **Martin Revill**. Like Gayne, he took on the role of both Membership Secretary and Treasurer. There was a six-month handover period when the two of them worked together. The opportunity to become involved in Society affairs under the guidance of Gayne was invaluable. Martin writes:

> 2003 was an eventful time to take over the job. The Council had decided the previous year that subscriptions should be increased in 2003. Nearly a third of members pay by banker's order and, inevitably, a large proportion of those members omitted to change their banking instructions. Many who pay by cheque still paid at the old rate. Hence, a fair amount of time and Society money was spent in bringing members' subscriptions up to date. Indeed, we still have some people each year paying by banker's order and also sending a cheque, hence paying twice. Then, inevitably, several people ring up to ask whether they have or have not paid.

There's never a dull moment! With proposals to increase subscriptions once again in 2009, I can only make a plea for members to pay up correctly and promptly. Use of a computer to keep the records up to date has helped enormously, particularly in maintaining the Society mailing list, but I have to admit also to keeping up to date the card index set up by Gayne, just in case! The most important and immediate task we have to address, as I see it, is to arrest the present decline in membership numbers. At the beginning of 2003 there were 964 members and these have fallen to 800 in 2008. If this decline is not reversed the Society may not exist in another 20 years!

Membership changes 1988 to 2008

year	net increase/decrease	total (end year)
1988	+214	214
1989	+36	250
1990	+100	350
1991	+100	450
1992	-90	340
1993	-30	310
1994	+53	363
1995	+82	445
1996	+40	485
1997	+98	583
1998	+57	640
1999	+110	750
2000	+86	836
2001	+95	931
2002	+33	964
2003	-57	907
2004	-44	863
2005	-53	812
2006	+44	856
2007	-28	828
2008	-28	800

THE SOCIETY'S LOGO

Philippa Davies

Image is important. Thus when we were designing our first Society stationery we knew that the letterhead needed to do us justice. Furthermore it needed to do our hero justice. JB's books were meticulously designed. The cover of *Ghastly Good Taste*, for example, reflected JB's early skill and eye for detail. His other books also showed particular care with their design and layout. Twenty years ago when the Society was formed we were conscious that the logo or image, whichever word is preferred, would be the first thing the eye would see on our letterheads and membership forms.

The first logo

None of the original Council members possessed layout and lettering talent but we were fortunate to know Ray Evison of the Kent Institute of Art and Design. He designed the JB monogram that adorned our letterheads for our first five years.

It was a fascinating lesson to see the large 'JB' drawn on graph paper in freehand and systematically reduced. The clean simplicity appealed.

Ray Evison's 'JB'

We took this artwork to Stan Wyatt of Thanet Printing Works in Ramsgate. He had worked with Jim Gibson for many years for the Hardy Society so we trusted his advice and we used Stan's layout and Ray's 'JB' for all our letterheads, membership forms, compliment slips and membership cards until 1994.

The costs and quantities of our initial order for stationery early in 1989 showed considerable confidence, considering there were no real members and therefore there was no real income. Our first invoice of March 1989 from Thanet Print was for:

Letterhead	1000	£34.00
Compliment Slips	1000	£27.00
Membership Cards (4 col)	1000	£29.00
Application Forms (B/W)	2000	£136.00

Luckily, the number of members, and therefore our funds, grew rapidly.

The second logo

As time went on we could identify our need for a slightly more distinctive logo for our flourishing society. Through observation of the setting of JB's books, interest grew in lettering, typography and calligraphy and in 1994 we were introduced by Betty Beale, one of our founder members, to Dr David Peace. He had been a friend of JB and a collaborator with him for the Staffordshire chapter in the *Collins Guide to English Parish Churches*. He was also an outstanding artist and a glass engraver.

David was so modest that he led one to believe his initial hesitation stemmed from a lack of ability. Rubbish, he was brilliant. The little gothic window for our logo began in David's home in Hemingford Abbots, Huntingdon. With a great deal of coaxing his pen moved and as we sat in his drawing room we watched the design take shape.

David Peace's 'JB'

David Peace at home in Hemingford Abbots designing the current logo

David Peace was schooled in Architecture at Sheffield University and became a Town Planner, ultimately in Cambridge. Latterly he developed his lifelong interest in lettering and glass engraving. There are many churches enhanced by his work. A fine example is the pair of glass doors at the West end of Westminster Abbey.

David likened the scrolls to ironwork and the crossed corners to 'a touch of old vicarage on a text'. This, too, began much larger, was tidied up and perfected, and was finally taken to a printer.

HISTORY: Printing & design

This time we went to Sebastian Carter, a printer recommended by David. Sebastian is the son of a 'father and son' business. David wrote: "He is the *only* printer. Anybody of quality goes to him. And afterwards forget the cost."

It was quite an adventure finding The Rampant Lion Press in Over, Cambridgeshire. Enclosed with his directions, Sebastian sent this note: "Incidentally you may be amused by the enclosed letter from the old boy (JB). I designed the Blond edition of *Ghastly Good Taste* in 1970 and he clearly liked it. Printer Carter is my father, Will, and he called my uncle John - Biblio Carter." Here is the text of JB's letter from Cloth Fair to Sebastian Carter:

Dear Printer Carter's Kid,
Wot a luvly job you have made of my jeu d'esprit of 38 years ago.
Ta & Ta again is the grateful remark of yours.
With best wishes to Printer Carter & all.
  John Betjeman

PS. First class choice of tints and paper.

Our bill for the stationery from Rampant Lion Press was:

Letterheads	500	£70.00
run on	500	£19.00
Membership cards	1000	£80.00
Membership forms	500	£450.00
run on	500	£85.00

We abandoned membership cards in the early 90's as they were just a nuisance to send out and served no purpose. Several from our original style still exist and collectors may like to ask for them.

David Peace's 'JB' has been used on all our printed material since 1994. His logo was adopted for the design of the gate to Betjeman Park in Wantage. In 1996 he was invited to execute the lettering for JB's memorial on the cartouche in Poets' Corner in Westminster Abbey. Its elegance harmonises with the rococo cartouche of more than two centuries earlier.

NEWSLETTERS & JOURNAL

Horace Liberty

For a society such as ours, it is important that there be good communication with members. At the beginning there were letters and flyers giving details of meetings and events and these soon developed into a regular *Newsletter*. The declared aim of the Newsletter is to "keep members in touch with what has happened or is about to happen in the world and study of Betjeman" – an essential function since not all members are able to attend society events in London or the Home Counties, or participate in a local branch of the society.

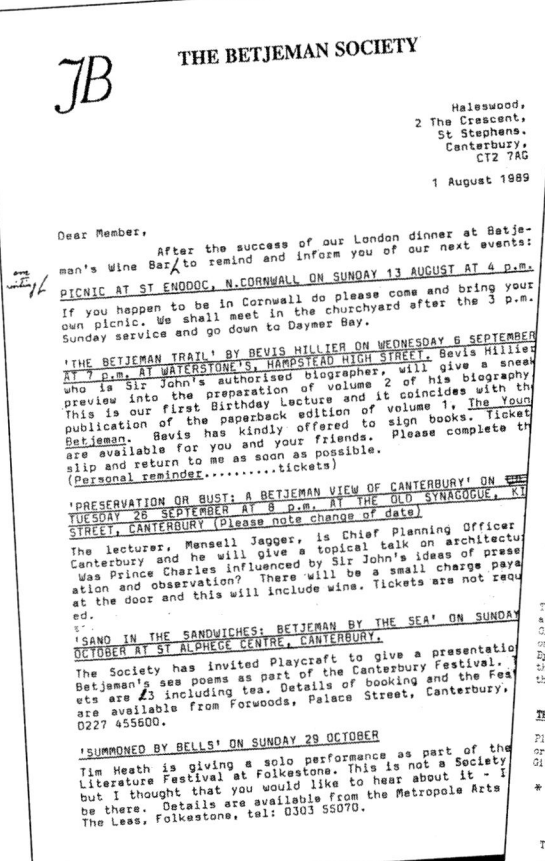

One of the first, and few, letter style Newsletters. Cut and paste took over.

HISTORY: *Publications*

Another early Newsletter prepared by Robert Shaw using cut and paste.

Progressing to John Cottenden's Desk Top Publishing method.

Recent Newsletters continue to give more publicity to links with other Societies

22 *A scrapbook of the first twenty years*

HISTORY: Publications

In addition to the *Newsletter*, there have been nineteen editions of our journal, *The Betjemanian*, which is published annually (as JB might have put it) "as a vital adjunct" to our society and its activities. The first edition appeared in December 1989 and reflected on the first year of The Betjeman Society, reporting the early events that we have read about elsewhere in this scrapbook.

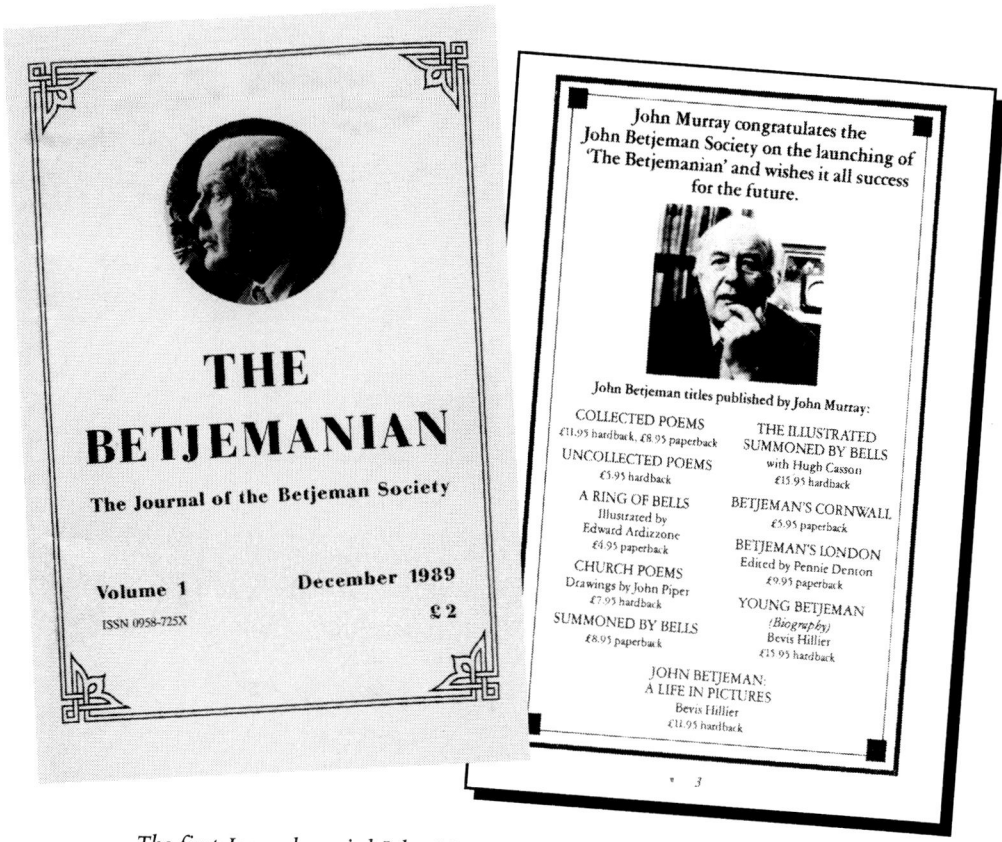

The first Journal carried John Murray's congratulations on its launch and advertised John Betjeman titles published by Murray

In his editorial for Volume 1, James Gibson, its first editor, set out the mission of our journal – "We want *The Betjemanian* to be very much the mouthpiece of Betjemanians so please support us ... by contributing your articles and letters, your bits of Betjeman news and any reminiscences you may have of him."

For me, it is those reminiscences of JB that are the particular joys to be found within the pages of our Journal:

> "I did enjoy the time I spent in John Betjeman's company .... Many times when I walked through the room where his "smalls" were hanging to dry he would invite me to "dodge the drips". On my last visit he gave me a copy of *Summoned by Bells* – now one of my greatest treasures." (Eileen Goff in *The Betjemanian* Volume 5, December 1993)

HISTORY: Publications

"Just look over there," he [JB] said.

I followed his gaze to a row of neatly stacked black high-powered motor cycles. Glistening in the sun, spotlessly clean, they looked magnificent.

"We don't need a taxi," he chuckled. "We'll go home on one of them. Just think of all that power between your legs!" He stood there almost helpless with laughter." (Reg Read in *The Betjemanian* Volume 1, December 1989)

"He wrote warmly and positively of empty churches and absent congregations, tolerantly of the redundant churches of Norwich, with sly wit of the Bishop ("When not entertaining, he's Maurice Norvic...") and movingly, in couplets, of old almshouse ladies in Jacobean cloaks." (Edward Mirzoeff in *The Betjemanian* Volume 19, 2008)

There have been four editors of *The Betjemanian* – James Gibson (Vols 1-2), Edward Griffin (Vols 3-5), Peter Gammond (Vols 6-17) and myself (Vols 18-19). The most daunting aspect of the editorial role is the need to maintain the high standard set by the previous editors who established not just a format, but a fascinating mix of news, reviews, articles and illustrations. In this respect, we must acknowledge the unstinting contribution of Peter Gammond over the years. His unrivalled knowledge of "all things Betjemanian" has proved a great asset to the society, not least in its publications. In the same way, from 1997 to 2006, John Cottenden set a standard for the *Newsletter* that was unrivalled in content and layout – a tradition continued by Michael Thomas until his recent, untimely death.

Publication of *The Betjemanian* and the *Newsletter* has enabled lectures and society events to be recorded and written up. Looking back through past copies is a bit like turning the pages of a photograph album - memories come flooding back and you seem to meet up with old friends again. Some of the events may be of only passing interest, but others, such as the annual lectures, are of more lasting significance and it is important that they do not disappear into the ether! In addition, within the pages, lists have been compiled, research findings published and occasionally permission has been granted to print a previously unpublished Betjeman poem. It is a source of amazement to me that invariably each year there are new books about Betjeman, or new editions of books by Betjeman, to be reviewed.

John Betjeman & the 'Mitford Girls'
The Betjemanian, Vol 17, 2006

HISTORY: Publications

Communication with the membership of The Betjeman Society is a two-way affair and our Journal and Newsletter encourage, in fact they are dependent upon, contributions from members.

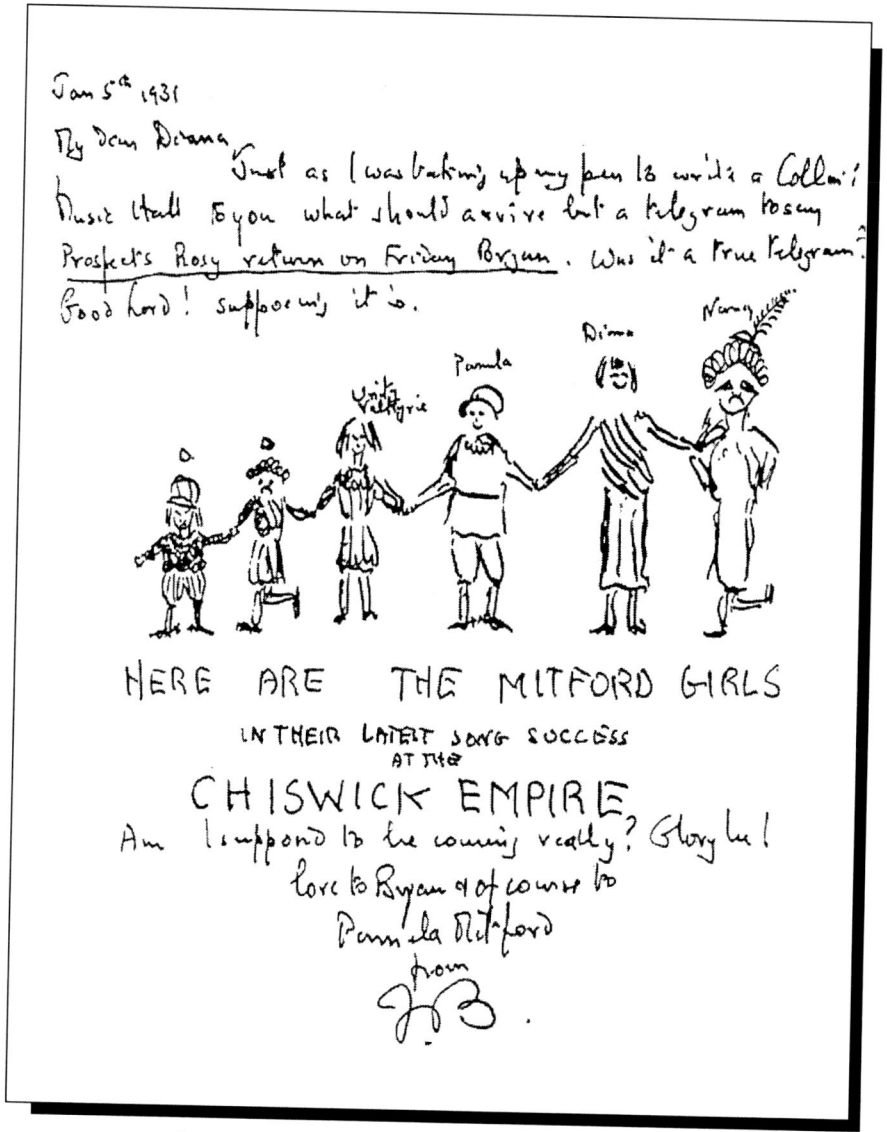

A letter from Betjeman to Diana Mitford written in 1931
Acknowledgements to The Betjeman Estate

The Betjemanian, Vol 17, 2006

Some of the contributors have featured regularly within the pages of our publications and we look forward to each edition so that we can enjoy their poetry, their insights, new discoveries and the fruits of their research. After twenty years, the Society's publications are still going strong and will continue to do so as long as there is the interest and contributions from our members to maintain them.

HISTORY: Publications

26 *A scrapbook of the first twenty years*

A BIBLIOGRAPHICAL COMPANION TO BETJEMAN

Peter Gammond

Our most significant contribution to the documentary promotion of John Betjeman's works has been this substantial volume which we published in 1997 in a limited edition of 250 copies to be sold to members only. As an inveterate collector in many literary and musical fields I had always liked listing things and, over my years as a freelance writer since 1960, have spent many hours compiling bibliographies of such subjects as Music-Hall, Jazz, Ragtime, Offenbach, Schubert, Mozart and British Poetry as offshoots of collecting books, music and memorabilia in all of these fields.

By the time I joined the Betjeman Society, soon after its beginnings, my listings of his work, mainly culled from the meagre bibliographies appended to various books, was looking quite impressive. Around 1995 I wrote to Betjeman's publisher John Murray and suggested that they might like to consider publishing a bibliography of the poet, hoping, in the normal course of events, that some money might be forthcoming to help me spend a bit more time on the project. Money for academic research is always around somewhere but available in amounts in inverse proportion to the popularity of the subject: a treatise on a subject in which virtually no-one is interested and which will sell about seventeen copies worldwide is well in line for a few thousand pounds. All the subjects in which I have been interested are considered popular and therefore of no interest to the providers of grants.

I was naturally disappointed when Murray's turned down the project: and somewhat discouraged when they told me they had been helping a researcher from the USA who was working on the Betjeman bibliography for the American branch of Oxford University Press. For the moment I dropped the idea of publication but went on compiling my list for my own interest.

I contacted the researcher in the USA to see whether the Betjeman Society could help him but merely got a cool response saying that he had everything he needed. I checked with OUP in Oxford, for whom I frequently work, to find out when the book would be coming out, but they knew nothing about it. By now, through contact with other Betjeman collectors like Philippa Davies, Mike Wilson, Ray Carter and John Heald, I had begun to realise that listing everything that Betjeman had written was not quite as simple as one might think.

His output was vast, varied and there was little to go by. The Margaret Stapleton Bibliography of 1972 which I came across was no more than a clue as to what a lot there was because she had, like the lady in white gloves, missed so much. But it provided a good start. Many other would-be bibliographers had simply given up.

My own MS was now pretty substantial but, perhaps mainly through looking at the scrapbook of cuttings (often undated) that John Heald had kept over the years, I began to get a clearer idea of what was involved. Some four years after my original Murray setback there was still no sign of the 'American Opus' and we made a firm decision to go ahead and complete our bibliography as far as we could in the time we could spare. We argued that it would be better to print something so that it might hopefully bring in masses of correspondence telling us what we had missed. Enlisting the invaluable co-operation of John Heald, there began a period of intensive research; some of it at Murray's, some at other likely sources, but most of it in the British Library's newspaper library at Colindale.

Colindale, to those who have not been there, is both a fascinating heap of accumulated knowledge and a frustrating and outdated machine. They do their best but it often takes ages to get hold of anything. Most newspapers are available only on ancient microfilms to be viewed on ancient machines which are either all in use at the time or not working. The main blockage came from the availability of only a couple of copying machines, for which there was always a long queue, and which kept on breaking down when you did get them and ultimately produced awful copies. Things that were in bound volumes of magazines, you could only have copied by proxy and have them sent to you for an excessive fee. There were also always other snags like Colindale having parking for only about ten cars, nearly always full, and just nowhere else on the streets to park for miles.

The ultimate decision to go ahead was pushed through by a whisker (strongly opposed by our President, a publisher who regarded us as rank amateurs in the bibliographical field, but strongly supported and aided by our Vice-President Candida Lycett Green). Those members who were interested enough in our effort to become subscribers, soon had the substantial results before them. The Bibliography was issued in 1997 at a cost of £30.00, available to members only.

We expected a lot more by way of addition and correction than we actually got. On the other hand we continued to research anyway and now have to consider how to disseminate the extra information we have. Of our 250 copies that were printed, around 50 must have gone their way as free copies (some obligatory) to libraries, institutions and a few important personages. The rest are now all sold and the Society, to the relief of the Council, especially me, made a reasonable profit. As I write this account I have just received a bookseller's catalogue in which a copy is offered for sale at £65.00. Perhaps we should have kept them all.

W.S. Peterson's Bibliography was published by Oxford University Press in 2006.

PRESIDENT

Bevis Hillier 2007

PAST PRESIDENTS

John G Murray CBE 1989 – 1993
Lord Horder 1994 – 1997
Lady Wilson 1998 – 2006

FOUNDER AND VICE-PRESIDENT

Philippa Davies 2000

VICE-PRESIDENTS

Candida Lycett Green 1995
John R Murray 1995
Frank Delaney 2001
Barry Humphries CBE 2001
Jonathan Stedall 2005
Edward Mirzoeff CVO CBE 2006

PAST VICE-PRESIDENTS

Bevis Hillier 1989-2006
Edred Wright 1990-2003
Dr James Gibson 1992-2005
Sir Hugh Casson CH 1995-1999
Kenneth Pinnock 1995-2008
David Peace MBE 1996-2002
Myfanwy Piper 1996-1998
Auberon Waugh 1996-2000
AN Wilson 1996-2006

John G Murray CBE
1989 – 1993
Philippa Davies

John (Jock) Murray, our Patron and first President, was a friend of JB and his publisher. They originally met through their 'alma mater', Magdalen College, Oxford.

Jock also became a friend of ours. It was quite some time before we met and he was tremendously friendly towards this faceless, fledgling society. We could not have anticipated what nature of response our first tremulous letter would receive. In fact we knew so little in those distant and ignorant days that we had to look in *Collected Poems* to find the name and address of its publisher and take a risk that there was a 'Mr Murray'.

Perhaps one of his letters to our membership secretary (Vicky Phillips) paints the best picture:

> Dear Mrs Phillips,
>
> The Betjemanian 2 is very splendid and very full of meat and fun except in one respect, for those who are on the verge of senility. In spite of all the talk of a new subscription, the present rate seems not to be mentioned and my memory is inadequate. So, I send £7.50 which seems most reasonable in view of the pleasures the Society provides and the size of the journal. Very noble of you to take on these burdens of membership.
>
> Yours sincerely
>
> *John G Murray*

This note was so typical of the many he sent us: amusing, kind and helpful and always adorned by carefully printed woodblock. Having been in contact only by post or telephone hitherto, he invited our Council to meet him one evening at 50 Albemarle Street. The moment of our arrival and of pressing the bell beside the iron railings and reading the polished brass plate is far more deeply etched in our memory than can be said of the inscription, engraved in a fading copperplate hand, announcing *Mr Murray*.

The entrance hall has its quirks too. The reception booth resembles a railway carriage or gipsy caravan and beyond that is a reading room cum waiting room, capped by a grand glass dome.

Jock Murray at No. 50 Albemarle Street

PEOPLE: *Past Presidents*

I am sure Jock was wondering what on earth we were like and we possibly hadn't realised how vital it was for our future that he approved of what he saw. Having entered a sophisticated and flamboyant world it came as no surprise to meet Jock, as we soon came to call the sixth Mr Murray. He appeared to fly towards us from his great height, bow tie, double cuffs and hair streaming out behind him. With his wife Diana at his side he greeted us in the middle drawing room and declared that, "as they say in the Colman family - if we are all mustered shall we begin". The beginning, as I recall it, was to be offered a glass of fine wine and then to be shown some of the Murray literary treasures: manuscripts, priceless first editions and portraits. For us the most amazing items were the Betjeman manuscripts, some unique and some with most amusing corrections by JB or his friends. And we still had charged glasses in our hands.

Waterstones, Hampstead - Bevis Hillier, Magda Rogers, Secretary to JB, and Jock Murray

Jock was so generous with his time and contacts and helped in countless ways: a few of the people he introduced us to as time went on were Bevis Hillier, Mervyn Horder, Ken Pinnock and his own son John, now Mr Murray VII. Luckily, Ken Pinnock joined the Council and always gave us unstinting help when asked.

We had invited Jock to be our Patron in recognition both of his role as JB's mentor and to make our group a little more august. Such was our inexperience that we considered Patron to be a suitable title. We only desired his moral support and never wished him to become the equivalent of a patron of the arts. He had, however, become rather attached to this title of Patron. He liked the idea of a pat on the back much more than the idea of the unsavoury duty of presiding over something. Soon after his acceptance, Ken Pinnock tactfully asked him to alter his title, in name

Jock Murray, in foreground, with members lining the stairs at Waterstones, Hampstead, for a sneak preview of Vol. 2 of Bevis Hillier's Betjeman biography, September 1989

A scrapbook of the first twenty years 31

only, and be called President. Luckily he accepted. That paved the way for, one day, being able to bestow the title of Vice-President on various other sympathetic worthies.

True to our word we never made great demands on him but he continued to help us almost to the day he died. He and Diana invited us to their wonderful home in Hampstead many times. Murray's forwarded numerous requests for membership or for information as our bank of knowledge and resource grew. They invited us to the launch of new publications and they kindly gave reductions on the cost of their books to the Society. Through his son, John, this happy state of affairs has continued and through John's wife, Virginia, we have been given the most generous access to Murray's archives for our research and publications.

It may appear that a great deal more is written in our Scrapbook about Jock than anyone else. We beg your indulgence and assure you that it is not intended to show preference. Simply, it is needed to cover the very important House of Murray.

Lord Horder
1994 – 1997
Philippa Davies

Our second President, Mervyn Horder, swept us off our feet from our first meeting. He sadly died in 1997, at the age of 86, but he gave us a good eight years of valued friendship. We shall particularly remember him for his recitals, reviews, editing journals and boosting membership. He had phenomenal energy. It seems impossible to think that he was in his late 70s when he came into our fold. From the word go, he came almost everywhere with us.

We organised a Cornish weekend with the Betjeman Centre at Wadebridge as the setting for our 4th birthday talk in 1992. At the eleventh hour our speaker, Gordon Kinsman Barker, had to go into hospital to be rescued from the most dreadful pain. Mervyn came to our aid. He had fortunately travelled down not only with his dinner jacket but also with his own recording of *Six Betjeman Songs*. After dinner he entertained us handsomely and those who were there will remember him, fleet of foot, strutting around on the parquet floor in the grand reception room at the Betjeman Centre.

He loved performing and wrote our programme for the Chelsea Arts Festival in 1993, he played the piano for singers at the Charing Cross Hotel in 1994 and he made an impassioned speech at the AGM in

Mervyn Horder at Wadebridge in 1992

32 *A scrapbook of the first twenty years*

the Globe Theatre museum in 1994, imploring us all to go out into the highways and byways and enlist more members - to enrol at least one each so as to bring our total up to one thousand.

His other plea was to reverse my decision to stand down from the Chair of the Council. Whether his power of persuasion was right I cannot say, but his persuasion worked. I must save for last a jewel in his crown which he shared with us in 1996. His talk on 'The Joys of Publishing' has been recorded in the Journal but how I wish I had it on tape. It was everything one could wish for from a talk - amusing, informative, well structured - a perfect vignette from a man of letters.

After our 'tea dance' at the Waldorf, we imagined we were quite welcome there and occasionally used it as a rendezvous. One day I arranged to meet Mervyn in the reception area. The staff could not have guessed that the man not overkeen on shaving, wearing a fisherman's smock and carrying a small smelly bundle of Arbroath smokies as a gift for me, was a 'Peer of the Realm'. They didn't mind who he was, they wanted him out. He took refuge in the pub next door where I found him telling his story.

On a more personal note, we shared many special days together. He searched Whitstable until he found a real sweet shop with sweets in jars. He searched Hythe for real ale and, once satisfied with the pub, he refused to sit with his back to the door.

Mervyn Horder encouraging Anthony Barnes to cut the cake at the Society's 7th birthday party, King's College, London, September 1995

Lord's cricket ground will never be the same again for us. We used to park in his Mews and I was entertained to lightly boiled eggs before the cricket match. Two pianos, one chair, numerous scripts, reviews and ever more entries for his common-place book, all around his open-plan living room were his markers of a fulfilling life. How generous he was in sharing his enthusiasms.

The Lady Wilson of Rievaulx
1998 – 2006
John Heald

We first met Lady Wilson at the unveiling of the memorial to JB in Poets' Corner in 1996. Then she accepted our invitation to speak to us at our 7th birthday party. She became our President at the Annual General Meeting in 1998 when the membership ratified Council's choice of her as the successor to Mervyn Horder. Council spent a lot of time thinking about this appointment but it is no secret that, once the name of Mary Wilson – The Lady Wilson of Rievaulx – was put forward, there was little doubt that she was the winner.

Presidents of this Society need have little in common, thank goodness, but one quality Mary Wilson shared with her predecessors, and surely this was the most important quality of all, is that she was just right for the job.

It cannot be easy to be the wife, or for that matter the husband, of a Prime Minister, but Lady Wilson managed to be both supportive and non-competitive without losing her own personality and talent or becoming no more than a Downing Street fixture and fitting. Sir John, in fact, had been quick to recognise that she was a true poet in her own right.

It was indeed at an official function that Betjeman and Mary Wilson first met – at the Royal Opera House in Covent Garden. The opera is not an interest we normally associate with Sir John. But I am sure he was glad he dressed up for that occasion for it led to what Candida describes as one of the most important and fruitful friendships of his life. They read together and went for walks in the park. Mary understood the melancholic side of Sir John's nature. She was an enduring help to him and it is not surprising that Candida chose her to unveil the Betjeman memorial in Westminster Abbey.

Mary Wilson with Peter Gammond, Basil Abbott, John Heald and Andrew Curtis at Diss, Norfolk, 2004

Lady Wilson had talked to us at our annual party in 1996, when she made a great impression with her recollections of her close friend. She is interested in our progress, joins us whenever possible and she likes to be kept informed of all our activities. She advises us, helps us but never interferes.

Mary Wilson said she was honoured, and of course we were honoured, when she accepted our invitation to be President. The Society is convinced that Sir John would be simply delighted to know she was our President, particularly so in his centenary year. She decided to step down at the end of that special year, 2006, and Bevis Hillier was invited to succeed her.

Letter to President & Vice-Presidents

Philippa Davies

The following letter and special questionnaire were sent to the President and Vice-Presidents of the Society in 2000. More recently appointed Vice-Presidents, Edward Mirzoeff and Jonathan Stedall, completed the questionnaire in February 2008.

Dear

Although 10 years does not seem long our memories are surprisingly short. Many time capsules were buried around the New Year to mark the Millennium. These may or may not have any meaning when they are exhumed in 50 or 100 years or more. It did make us realise that the time was ripe for us to gather and share our own history and record the first precious years of The Betjeman Society. I have set myself the task of gathering all I can. We shall have contributions from many people and we are hoping for a lively, informative little book. It may be of some use to other societies if they are floundering in the dark as we once were though I expect it will really be a parochial publication.

We have often depended upon you, our President and Vice-Presidents, for wisdom and support. Normally the members see you in a list as honorary and decorative. Now we would like you to have the opportunity to reveal yourselves and let us hear what you have to say. That is why I am writing to you all now. All the VPs I have spoken to think it is a super idea.

Please could I ask you for a small contribution? This is meant to be a simple task perhaps to be done over a cup of coffee today or tomorrow. I have thought out some questions and spaced them out so you can just fill in the gaps. If you have more to say on any part, feel free to attach another sheet. This is the pattern that I have in mind but it is not binding.

With thanks and all best wishes

PJD

THE BETJEMAN SOCIETY SPECIAL QUESTIONNAIRE

How did you come across the Betjeman Society?

What do you remember of your first meeting?

Please could you tell us your favourite poem by Betjeman and add a few lines about the reason for your choice?

Which is your favourite piece of prose?

Could you name your favourite Betjeman site or building or place?

A character like Betjeman leaves us with many memories. Would you share with us your personal favourite?

As we look to the future what ideas do you have for Betjeman's work or that of the Society?

[NB In response, Lady Wilson chose to write her own answers in the form of a letter.]

Responses to letter and questionnaire
Lady Wilson's letter

We are all grateful to Sir John Betjeman for sharing with us "The bonus of laughter". The popular concept of him is of a writer of pleasing poetry, full of fun, and a light-hearted observer of the passing scene. But he was, as are we all, a complex character, often full of self-doubt, particularly about his work - "But is it any good?" and prone to occasional anxieties and depressions. I am confident that he had a very strong religious faith but, even there, doubt would creep in, as in the splendid *Christmas* poem - *And is it true? That most tremendous tale of all.* And often pathos would creep into his poems, as in *Sudden illness at the bus-stop*.

My friendship with John Betjeman was based on a love of poetry and the joy of being able to 'talk poetry' with a friend, particularly as we were both involved in so many different things. John was extremely hard-working, sitting on committees, attending meetings, all outside his working day. Sometimes he would call on me at tea-time and say "Let's have some poetry - what about a bit of Wordsworth, or Tennyson?" He liked long narrative poems (one afternoon I read him the whole of *Maud*!) so I would start to read and often, after a few verses, would look up and find him fast asleep. I would read on for my own pleasure to the end of the poem, when he would awaken, refreshed!

Everyone knows John the poet, but not everyone remembers his interest in and his knowledge of architecture. He taught a generation to look with a new eye at Victorian buildings, particularly those we had learned to despise. He was very knowledgeable about these buildings, knowing and naming the architects. He taught me to 'look up' at the upper storeys and roofs of buildings and to enjoy the detail in them - try that in, say, Oxford Street - it's a revelation! My son was driving him once and had a perilous trip, as John would persist in exclaiming and pointing out buildings on the way.

He always gave his support to the preservation of threatened buildings.

I remember he was delighted with an extraordinary building I pointed out to him on the Embankment, which has a plethora of turrets, staircases and cupolas. He knew that it had been designed by two architects and invented an imaginary conversation between them:

> *"Don't you think that wall looks a bit plain?"*
> *"Yes, what about another window, turret, tower?"*

John dealt daily with an enormous postbag, often writing long letters by hand. He was always encouraging to budding poets, never unkindly critical. Sometimes he would murmur comments as I was reading to him - "Tautology perhaps?" or once "No, no! Weak Swinburne!" As you can imagine <u>that</u> offering went straight into the bin!

John Betjeman was, and still is, our much-loved Poet Laureate.

Philippa Davies

How did you come across The Betjeman Society?
The idea just came out of the top of my head. I was desperate to obtain tickets for JB's Memorial Service and I felt my letter of application had to be somewhat embroidered and noticeable. I willingly admit to performing this mild act of imposture.

What do you remember of your first meeting?
Sheer enjoyment of reading and sharing favourite poems with a group of like-minded people.

Favourite poem
The Subaltern's Lovesong. This is the first poem I ever really enjoyed and I came across it in Hultons series of Pocket Poets, the only poetry book I had hitherto voluntarily opened. It became the 'key' that opened my mind to other poems by JB and then to other poets. That book is one of the treasures of my collection.

Favourite prose
The introduction to the *Collins Guide to English Parish Churches*, particularly the longest sentence on page 31.

Favourite place
All parish churches. I am so grateful to have been encouraged to look above me and around me sometimes with humour but always, now, with a more discerning eye.

Favourite memory
One of my great disappointments is that I never did meet JB. But I loved him on the wireless and on the television.

Ideas for the future
To encourage the formation of more Branches. To encourage members to learn poetry by heart.

Frank Delaney

How did you come across The Betjeman Society?
Can't remember

Favourite poem
A Subaltern's Lovesong. That was my introduction to him. I saw it in an Observer article about Joan Hunter Dunn.

Favourite place
St Pancras, St Botolph's.

Favourite memory
Him saying on television (when asked about life's regrets) "I haven't had enough sex".

Ideas for the future
More public awareness - repetitions of the works.

James Gibson

How did you come across The Betjeman Society?
By reading about the opening meeting in the Canterbury newspaper.

What do you remember of your first meeting?
That my wife had told me that in view of my extensive commitments to the Hardy Society (I was editor of the Journal), I was on no account to take on any further responsibilities. She was remarkably good-tempered when I returned home and told her I had agreed to be Chairman and to be Editor of the Betjemanian. (In fact memory condenses and we can safely say he did have a cooling-off period before happily volunteering. PJD)

Favourite poem
I have many favourites but if I can take only one to my Desert Island it would be *Old Friends*: an evocative mixture of the detailed and the universal - nostalgic but not sentimental. It touches the heart.

Favourite prose
The Lecture - so true to one's own experiences.

Favourite place
St Enodoc Church.

Favourite memory
A meeting of the Society in St Enodoc churchyard.

Ideas for the future
Just to continue spreading the message of JB's many writings and videos to the English-speaking public, which is much in need of his humour, common sense, hatred of the vulgar and meretricious, and love of life.

Bevis Hillier

How did you come across The Betjeman Society?
Not sure. Did Jock Murray tell me? Was I approached to give a talk?

What do you remember of your first meeting?
Very perceptive questions from the audience after I gave my lecture.

Favourite poem
Indoor Games near Newbury - brilliant versification; a lost age perfectly conjured up; much humour and satire, but also tenderness in the treatment of that love you feel as a child. This is the sort of thing that Betjeman does better than any other poet, before or since.

Favourite prose
Port Isaac in *First and Last Loves*.

Favourite place
Holly Village, Highgate - Gothic Revival with a touch of Charles Addams.

Favourite memory
After a lunch with much wine, walking back with him to his Chelsea house. I began by reciting *Indoor Games*. Rather tickled, I think, that I had bothered to learn it by heart, he joined in.

Ideas for the future
A grand British Museum or British Library exhibition for the centenary of his birth, 2006, please. And *The Friends of the Cathedral* to be added to a new edition of Collected Poems.[It was.] A Betjeman Room at Magdalen College, like the Max Beerbohm Room at Merton College.

Candida Lycett Green
What do you remember of your first meeting?
An ethereal night in the City (Butchers Hall, 21st November 1998) with not a place unfilled and good beef and everything glittering.

Favourite poem
Upper Lambourne because it was my Mum's favourite and because I know and love the place and love the pastoral quality of the poem.

Favourite prose
Kelmscott. Again because I know and love the place but this adds an extra layer.

Favourite place
Trebetherick, where else.

Favourite memory
Eating crisps in pub gardens in the sunshine as a child while he (JB) had a "nip" inside.

Ideas for the future
Keep up the good work.

Edward Mirzoeff
How did you come across The Betjeman Society?
I attended the London gathering at Betjeman's Restaurant, Cloth Fair.

What do you remember of your first meeting?
The lively and enthusiastic "Betjeman Girl" who seemed to be the driving force – one Philippa Davies ....

Favourite poem
Death of King George V is one – a perfect lyric, moving and with such strong imagery. *Devonshire Street W1* is another – so characteristically gloomy.

Favourite prose
Lisland

Favourite place
The Chiltern Court Restaurant, with its memories of Metroland. Of course it no longer exists. Or *The Orchard*, Chorleywood.

Favourite memory
There are too many for this space – but see my notes to the DVDs of *Metroland* and *A Passion for English Churches* (the latter to appear in slightly different form in the Betjemanian).

Ideas for the future
The Society has to be more active, and to attract a whole new generation if it is to survive in the long run. I should like to see more events in the programme, for a start. Why, for example, has no-one set up a debate between Bevis Hillier and A.N.Wilson about their differing approaches to Betjeman? Might have attracted a little interest from outside. Or a talk by Elizabeth Cavendish and a visit to Chatsworth? Or a screening of my biographical film of 2001? Or a talk by Edward Roberts, who edited so many of JB's films?

John Murray
How did you come across The Betjeman Society?
I simply cannot remember that far back.

Favourite poem
Apart from *Summoned by Bells, Executive*. I saw these all round me as I travelled the country as a publisher's rep. and always longed for the 'maître d' hotel' to allow <u>me</u> to sign the bill! <u>My</u> Aston Martin was a Mini. On a more thoughtful note, *Death in Leamington*. It has an immediacy and gentleness that leaves a deep and lasting impression.

Favourite prose
St Endellion.

Favourite place
Building: Sir Gilbert Scott's St Pancras Station Hotel -

Landscape: The view across from St Enodoc to the sea -

Favourite memory
Walking round Smithfield, with JB stopping at each shop to point out some little detail with infectious enthusiasm. The whole place came alive peopled with the clergy of St Bart. the Great, the periwig makers whose shops were built <u>into</u> the church, the gentle Augustinian nuns who tended Wat Tyler after he was stabbed and gems such as Hogarth's huge murals in the hospital. As everyone knows, going for a walk with JB was an experience never forgotten.

Ideas for the future
Continue to fight for the human element in everything.

David Peace
How did you come across The Betjeman Society?
Through Betty Beale. I engraved a church window for her as a memorial to her husband.

What do you remember of your first meeting?
Probably being inveigled! I am not habitually an attendee of meetings.

Favourite poem
How to Get on in Society is one favourite. Another is *A Shropshire Lad*. I remember JB reciting this at my house in a spoof Midlands accent.

Favourite prose
Articles about churches in his series for The Daily Telegraph.

Favourite place
The fun of going round Staffordshire together, compiling the list for that chapter in the Collins Guide to Parish Churches. One memorable day we screeched to a halt when JB unexpectedly exclaimed "Look, a ruined Bodley". True enough, it was.

Favourite memory
Watching JB roaring with laughter at some remark made by my wife, Jean.

Kenneth Pinnock

How did you come across The Betjeman Society?
Jock Murray told me of its formation. I think he showed me Philippa's letter. Then I got in touch with my old friend Jim Gibson.

What do you remember of your first meeting?
The first meeting I recall was the first AGM at the Dominican Priory in Canterbury, when we suffered a gas attack in two waves and nearly had to evacuate the building.

Favourite poem
An impossible question but I'll nominate *Westgate on Sea* because it appeals to my strong sense of local patriotism.

Favourite prose
The chapter on the 'mutilated masterpieces': Blackfriars, Holborn Viaduct and Cannon Street, in *London's Historic Railway Stations*. It wonderfully evokes the high-Victorian 'mighty dream' of the railways as annihilators of distance and their terminus hotels as haunts of luxury. Of Blackfriars, JB says "The style is Italian, no doubt to give a European touch to the passer-by. Cut into the heavily rusticated brick pilasters, which adorn this façade, are the names of principal stations reached by the S.E. and C.R., Baden-Baden and Beckenham, Bremen and Broadstairs, Brindisi and Bromley, Ramsgate and Leipzig, Sittingbourne and Marseilles, Westgate-on-Sea and St Petersburg, Walmer and Wiesbaden, they flank the entrances with bewildering supplication unnoticed by the sad commuters hurrying to queue in the echoing woodwork of the booking hall. It was in this booking hall that I asked for a return to St Petersburg and was referred to Victoria Continental".

Favourite place
The middle drawing room at 50 Albemarle Street, John Murray's office, where I saw JB one December morning, on one of his many visits, addressing his Christmas cards under the watchful eye of Archibald who sat propped in one corner.

PEOPLE: *Presidents & Vice-Presidents' Questionnaire*

Favourite memory
Perhaps what I have just written in answer to the last question. But running it very close is Christopher Nicholson's story of how JB asked him to say what the new book by David Newsome (Headmaster of Christ's Hospital, where Nicholson then was teaching English) was all about. In a few crisp sentences Nicholson summarised Newsome's argument that basically humankind can be divided between those who take an Aristotelian or a Platonic view of life. JB's reaction was a few moments of stunned silence, and then 'My God! Have some more champers'.

Ideas for the future
As to Betjeman's works, I hope that scholars will keep them alive by discussing them and I'm sure that others will do so simply by reading and enjoying them. As to the Society, any ideas of mine about its future activities would seem poor stuff by comparison with the immense range and inventiveness that have characterised the last ten years.

Jonathan Stedall

How did you come across The Betjeman Society?
An invitation from Kay Jackman in Sherborne.

What do you remember of your first meeting?
A walk on Greenaway in Trebetherick to discuss the making of a series of films for TWW - my first job as a director - and the ease at which JB accepted an inexperienced 23 year old, and his delight that I was an 'Old Harrovian'.

Favourite poem
A Child Ill - because of its wonderful combination of JB's anxiety and his compassion. Also *Christmas* because of all the question marks.

Favourite prose
A letter written to me in 1966 when I was considering leaving my work in television for a teaching career. He put such decisions into perfect perspective.

Favourite place
Dog Mess Walk (alias Radnor Walk, Chelsea) where I spent so many happy times with John and Elizabeth Cavendish.

Favourite memory
A very dull and tiring journey by coach across Romania when, towards the end of the day and out of the silence, came John's voice – 'I <u>am</u> enjoying the boredom'.

Ideas for the future
The priority must surely be to bring his poetry and his biography to the attention of younger people who have no memory of him, and have little experience of what a true celebrity is. The Society must, therefore, resist being solely a haven for nostalgia and instead try to communicate as energetically and creatively as the great man himself.

Auberon Waugh

How did you come across The Betjeman Society?
Can't remember.

What do you remember of your first meeting?
A memorable collection of all the nicest and least pretentious people in London, nobody showing off, all sharing a genuine enjoyment.

Favourite poem
Slough I am afraid, but also *Subaltern's Lovesong*.

"And get that man with double chin/ Who'll always cheat and always win,/ Who washes his repulsive skin/ In women's tears." A genuine, deeply felt anger and true emotion brilliantly expressed.

Favourite place
<u>Not</u> anything neo-Gothic or C19. He loved the real thing too cf. Longleat.

Favourite memory
1) How exceptionally friendly he was to an 8-year-old, seeming to prefer the company of children.

2) Literally rolling on the floor with laughter in a public house on Ludgate Circus at a long-forgotten joke I had made. The proudest moment of my life.

Ideas for the future
Spread knowledge of the work wherever possible, pointing out that the modern movement has failed and it is time to look for poetry that rhymes, scans and makes sense.

AN Wilson
How did you come across The Betjeman Society?
Introduced to it by Philippa Davies the 'echt' Betjeman woman.

What do you remember of your first meeting?
The most memorable meeting was the unveiling of the beautiful memorial in Westminster Abbey.

Favourite poem
St Saviours, Aberdeen Park, Highbury is one of my favourites. The longer time goes on the more JB seems to me a supreme religious poet. This poem conveys his piety - and love of North London where I live.

Favourite prose
Port Quin entry in his Shell guides to Cornwall: a prose poem about a fishing village in which all the men were shipwrecked.

Favourite place
I have come to love Daymer Bay in North Cornwall - he lies buried at the top of the bay in St Enodoc churchyard, with seaside golf going on all round him.

Favourite memory
Alas we met only once. He roared with laughter about Thomas Crapper, inventor of the "flush" and said his idea of sexual bliss was to be given a real wigging by Lady Harrod.

Edred Wright

How did you come across The Betjeman Society?

Through the founder.

What do you remember of your first meeting?

It was rather an informal (the first house group) meeting and I couldn't really remember why I was there.

(Edred, you are far too modest, it was probably your shout of enthusiasm when I mentioned an evening of JB which encouraged me more than anything else to gather a group of friends for an informal evening. PJD)

Favourite poem

Westminster Abbey as I have been closely associated with that place for most of my life (as a chorister and assisting with music for the coronation).

Favourite place

Westminster Abbey because of the wonderful plaque in his memory.

10th Aniversary Dinner, Butcher's Hall, 1998. Left to right: Peter Gammond, Philippa Davies, Gerry Bishton, Edred Wright, John Cottenden, Mary Wilson, Jim Gibson, John Heald, Candida Lycett Green, Gayne Wells, Shirley Dex, Bevis Hillier & John Murray.

Picture by kind permission of Picture Partnership

OFFICERS OF THE BETJEMAN SOCIETY

Chairman
David Pattison

James Gibson	1988-1991	Peter Gammond	1997-2002
Philippa Davies	1991-1997	John Heald	2002-2008

Vice-Chairman
John Heald

Edred Wright	1988-1990	Philippa Davies	1997-1999
Robert Shaw	1990-1994	John Heald	1999-2002
Jonathan Fryer	1994-1995	Peter Gammond	2002-2008
Peter Gammond	1995-1997		

Secretary
Colin Wright

Philippa Davies	1988-1990	John Heald	1994-2002
Kenneth Pinnock	1990-1994	Andrew Curtis	2002-2005

Treasurer
Martin Revill

Jake Davies	1988-1994	Gayne Wells	1997-2003
Rev. Gerry Bishton	1994-1997		

Membership Secretary
Martin Revill

Vicky Phillips	1988-1993	Gayne Wells	1994-2003
James Luly	1993-1994		

Editor of the Betjemanian
Horace Liberty

James Gibson (Vols 1-2)	1989-1990	Peter Gammond (Vols 6-17)	1995-2006
Edward Griffin (Vols 3-5)	1991-1994		

Editor of the Newsletter
Steven Jackson

Philippa Davies (1-5)	1989-1990	John Cottenden (32-67)	1998-2006
Robert Shaw (6-31)	1990-1998	Michael Thomas (69-72)	2007-2008

BETJEMAN COUNCIL MEMBERS

		Elected	*To*
BISHTON	Gerry	1994	2000
BLACKLOCK	Peter	1990	1993
COTTENDEN	John	1993	2006
COVER	Sue	1990	1991
CURTIS	Andrew	2001	2005
DAVIES	Jake	1988	1994
DAVIES	Philippa	1988	2000
DEX	Shirley	1995	2000
FRYER	Jonathan	1992	1997
GAMMOND	Peter	1993	Continues
GIBSON	Helen	1988	1991
GIBSON	James	1988	1991
GRIFFIN	Edward	1991	1994
GRIFFIN	Margaret	1991	1996
HEALD	John	1994	Continues
LANGFORD	John	2000	2004
LAWRENCE	Philippa	1997	2004
LOWRY	Ian	2008	Continues
LULY	James	1993	1994
PATTISON	David	2006	Continues
PEACH	John	1995	1996
PHILLIPS	Vicky	1988	1993
PINNOCK	Kenneth	1990	1994
REVILL	Martin	2001	Continues
ROLLASON	Jean	2008	Continues
SHAW	Robert	1989	1994
SIMPSON	Diane	1999	2001
STAREY	Martin	1988	1990
TAYLOR	Helen	1988	1991
THOMAS	Michael	2007	2008
THORNE	Anthony	1997	1998
WARD	Ian	1988	1989
WELLS	Gayne	1993	2003
WIGMORE	Paul	1992	1993
WILCOCKSON	Andrew	1993	1995
WILSON	Michael	2000	2006
WRIGHT	Colin	2005	Continues
WRIGHT	Edred	1988	1991

Branch History

John Cottenden   Branch co-ordinator, 1995-2006
(written by John Cottenden in 2000)

'Large streams from little fountains flow
Tall trees from little acorns grow'

This is the story of the Betjeman Society since the seeds of its first two Branches were sown in 1989 in **Sherborne**, by Kay Jackman and in **Bristol** by Bill Pickard. These were followed later by Branches in **Canterbury**, **Birmingham** and **Oxford University**.

Of the early Branches **Sherborne** and **Canterbury** are still very active. **Bristol,** and later **Weston-Super-Mare**, failed to survive following the resignation through ill health of the organiser, Bill Pickard. **Birmingham** led by Jo Hunt, ceased for the same reason and **Oxford University** through lack of a President.

A Branch was formed in **Ireland** following a society visit in 1994. Unfortunately, since the death last year of its originator, George Peche, this Branch has ceased to operate. Others however have taken their place and now in the year 2000 the Society can boast seven established Branches.

When I was given the task of branch co-ordinator in 1995 I realised that I could not create Branches of the Society. I could only help by supporting those that were established by representing their interests at Council meetings and seeing that encouragement was given to those members wishing to start one.

The creation of a Branch has no set formula. The Society cannot take a map, point to a town and say "we will form a Branch there" and then descend, like recruiting officers, signing up members.

Although the Society can offer initial financial assistance and moral support, the prime effort has to come from an individual or a group of members, guided by a desire to spend some of their spare time in the company of others of like mind enjoying the works of Sir John Betjeman. How this time is used differs from Branch to Branch.

Canterbury enjoy their regular Saturday morning poetry readings and the occasional Branch Dinner. **Sherborne** raise considerable sums of money for charity with their many public performances of Betjeman poetry. The **Shires** are entirely different with their enthusiastic and ambitious programme of tours, lectures, readings and a sparkling Branch journal. **Wantage** and **Oxford** both enjoy a quieter life with readings, visits and occasional social events. The Society's two newest branches, the *Isle of Man* and *Lincolnshire*, have found their feet and now hold regular meetings and events.

An important factor to bear in mind when starting a Branch is that like plants in the early stages of their growth, they are fragile. Whilst it is essential to have an enthusiastic organiser to start up a Branch, it is of double importance to have active members to strengthen it and make it grow. One of the reasons behind the demise of the branches mentioned earlier was simply that following the loss of their organiser there was no one willing to pick up the baton and carry on.

The strengthening of the Society's Branch network is important to its growth for several reasons. It provides a meeting-point for members who cannot always attend distant main Society events. It encourages the exploration of Betjeman-related subjects at a local level. Above all it makes an individual member feel included and not just a figure sending in an annual subscription to a remote organisation. A recent example of the value of the Branches to the Society has been the hosting of the last two AGMs by the *Shires* and *Sherborne* respectively. Both occasions were brilliantly organised and succeeded in attracting double the turnout of members that were at some previous AGMs.

In looking to the future one would like to see London added to the Branch network. In order to complete the geographic pattern, Cornwall, the West Midlands and the Northern Counties would be required. Let us hope that somewhere in those areas there are enterprising members who can turn this wish into reality.

Summary

The first Branch of the Betjeman Society was formed in Sherborne, Dorset, in 1989 within months of the inaugural meeting of the main Society in Canterbury. Since then, although ten more were established in the next 10 years, there are, currently, only eight - all in England - and there are no Branches of the Society in Ireland, Wales, Scotland or overseas.

BRANCH	ESTABLISHED	CLOSED
Sherborne	1989	
Bristol/Weston Super Mare	1989	1997
Canterbury	1990	
Birmingham	1991	1998
Oxford University	1990	1995
Wantage	1995	
Ireland	1995	1999
Oxford	1996 refounded 2006	
The Shires	1997	
Isle of Man	1999	
Lincolnshire	1999	
Ridings	2008	

Sherborne Branch

Kay Jackman (Chairman) writes:

Going to Cornwall in August 1989 and visiting St Enodoc church in Trebetherick, I found a brochure from Canterbury announcing the formation of the main Society. At home, I advertised for anyone interested in Betjeman's poetry and from there the Sherborne branch grew, reading and talking about JB.

Attendance at meetings and performances: from few to over 100. Branch membership: many that pay and masses that don't pay.

Schools and churches heard of our existence and invited us to give recitals in the local area and further afield. Proceeds were always given to charities - for Cancer, Parkinson's Disease and churches. In this way we have raised thousands of pounds.

Lord (Mervyn) Horder came with the Sherborne group to Cerne Abbas in November 1993 when we were raising money for the 'church tower' fund and Jonathan Stedall came to the Society's AGM in Sherborne in 2000. On the evening before that meeting, where he was the principal guest, he showed us pictures of himself with JB looking around Sherborne as well as his favourite haunts in Cornwall.

John Heald, Kay Jackman, Peter Gammond and Jonathan Stedall at the AGM in Sherborne, 2000

A great occasion was when HRH The Prince of Wales came to a programme of poems with musical interludes presented by the Sherborne branch at St Mary's Church, Dorchester on 14th December 2001. From that very special event, sponsored by the main society, we raised £4,000 in aid of 'Breakthrough Breast Cancer'.

Miss Greig was a former churchwarden at Donhead St Mary, Wiltshire, who made herself known to us at the end of one of our Betjeman readings in the church there in

BRANCHES: *History*

> In aid of Breakthrough Breast Cancer
>
> **breakthrough**
> breast cancer
> Registered Charity No. 0162636
>
> ## MOMENTS OF VISION
>
> In the Presence of His Royal Highness
> THE PRINCE OF WALES
>
> A programme of poems
> presented by
> THE BETJEMAN SOCIETY
> *(Sherborne Branch)*
> with Musical Interludes
> at St. Mary's Church, Edward Road,
> DORCHESTER
> Friday, 14th December, 2001 at 5.30 pm
>
> <u>Audience to be seated by 5.00 pm</u>
>
> Admission by programme £10
> from: The Music Box, Princes Street, Dorchester
>   Dorset, DT1 1RL. Telephone 01305 264216
> and: The Tourist Information Centre
>   Digby Road, Sherborne. Telephone 01935 815341

HRH The Prince of Wales at a performance of 'Moments of Vision' at St Mary's church, Dorchester, in December 2001

October 2005. She remembers meeting JB many times; as the keyholder she would unlock the church and sit outside reading her book while he looked round admiring the interior. When he came out he would say "We really have enjoyed ourselves."

50   *A scrapbook of the first twenty years*

Miss Sue Greig at Donhead St Mary in 2005

A Betjeman evening at St. Mary's Church, Alvediston, June 2008

AN EVENING OF READINGS

from the works of

SIR JOHN BETJEMAN

performed (with music) by the Sherborne Branch of the Betjeman Society

in aid of St Mary's Restoration Appeal

Friday 13 June

7.00pm

St Mary's Church, Alvediston

* tickets: £5 (incl wine after the performance)
* a donations box will towards the Restoration Appeal will be placed at the Church door
* seating up to 90 – please book early

Canterbury Branch

After a meeting early in 1990 at the King's School, Canterbury, to test local interest, the Canterbury branch of the Betjeman Society was formed. Its first co-ordinator was the **Revd. Robert LLoyd** who was, incidentally, related to Peggy Purey-Cust [JB's first and purest love – see *Summoned by Bells*].

Nine years later, he wrote:
Several local people were being introduced to one another on that evening and they decided to found a very happy little branch of the new Society. Ever since then we have met in one another's homes on the first Saturday of each month (except August). We remain a small group of about a dozen with several people coming since we started. The temptation is to try to grow, but we have to remember that the rooms of most people cannot hold more than our present number. To have to move to a hall would not give the meetings the same feel in any way. But we do indeed welcome new members when they come along. And then some move away and others die.

Of our members, Mary Nugent thinks she may be the only one to have met JB. She met him at a Harrods tea party to promote his *Collected Poems*. "We had a lovely chat" Mary says "and then he drew a champagne glass incorporating his autograph on my copy. I wonder if any other members of the Society have champagne glasses gracing their books?"

We give thanks in East Kent for our 9 years together and look forward with hope to the future. Perhaps John Keats can have the last word:

BRANCHES: *History*

> THE
> BETJEMAN SOCIETY
> Presents
>
> POETS LAUREATE
>
> and the launch of
> The Canterbury Branch
> of the
> Betjeman Society
>
> AT: The Old Synagogue, King Street, Canterbury
> ON: Thursday January 31st at 7.30 pm.
>
> Please bring your own choices of any Laureate.
>
> No tickets required — small charge for small refreshments.

The launch of the Canterbury branch, 31st January 1990

Sweet are the pleasures that to verse belong
But doubly sweet a brotherhood in song.

Robert LLoyd was succeeded by **Patricia Mann** in 2000. She reports that:
"The life and poetry of John Betjeman was our common interest. We found that we shared a general love of poetry and would occasionally invite a visiting speaker, such as John Heath Stubbs to our meetings. Over the past twenty years we have also gone on to study other poets like Clare, Thomas Hardy, Tennyson, Robert Frost and Christina Rossetti. Poetry about counties, rivers. emotions, dreams, the sea, celebrations, war, families, creatures, joy and many, many more subjects have been read and enjoyed.

Revd. Robert LLoyd celebrating the 10th anniversary of the Canterbury Branch

At present we have fourteen members. We help when AGMs and other Society events take place in Canterbury. Some of us also perform as the Betjeman Players at Canterbury festivals and give poetry recitals locally - as in Patrixbourne, ten miles from Canterbury, in 2003.
JB wrote a letter to the church in Patrixbourne saying how much he liked it. The letter is framed and hangs at the southwest end of the church near the door."

52   *A scrapbook of the first twenty years*

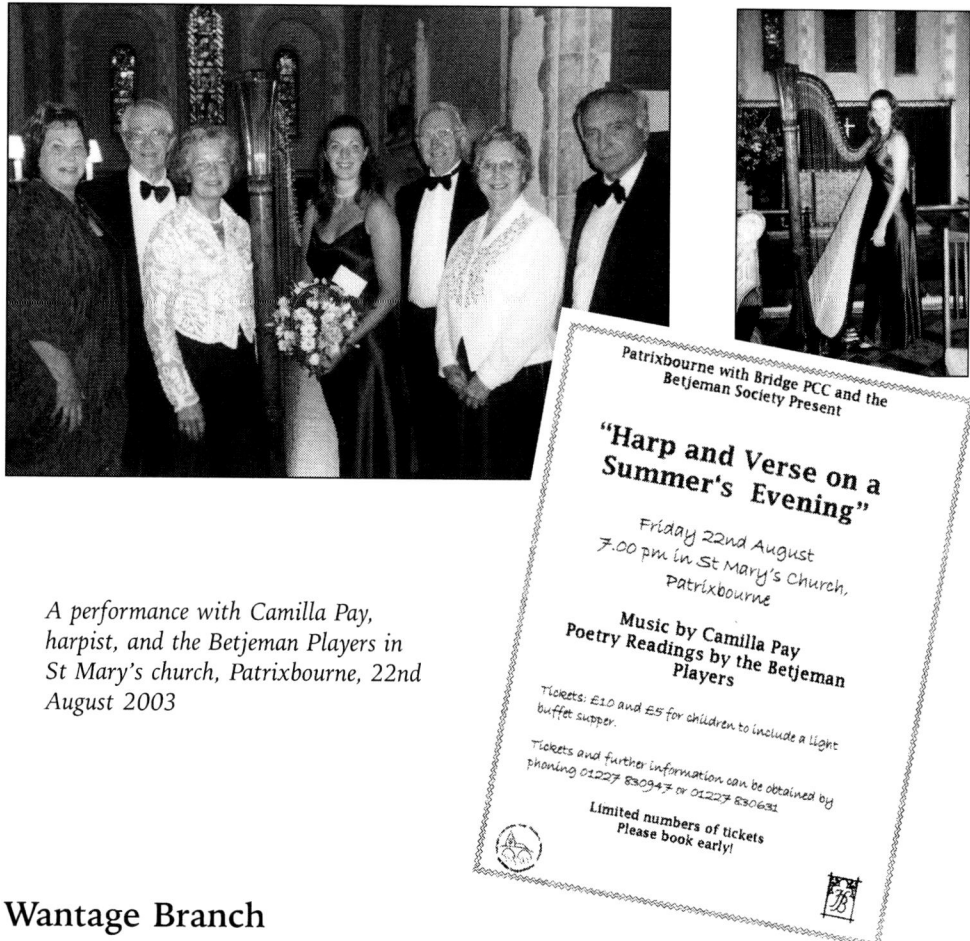

A performance with Camilla Pay, harpist, and the Betjeman Players in St Mary's church, Patrixbourne, 22nd August 2003

Patrixbourne with Bridge PCC and the Betjeman Society Present

"Harp and Verse on a Summer's Evening"

Friday 22nd August
7.00 pm in St Mary's Church, Patrixbourne

Music by Camilla Pay
Poetry Readings by the Betjeman Players

Tickets: £10 and £5 for children to include a light buffet supper.

Tickets and further information can be obtained by phoning 01227 830947 or 01227 830631

Limited numbers of tickets
Please book early!

Wantage Branch

Pat Mattimore (Membership Secretary and Treasurer) writes:

"We are very fortunate in the Wantage Branch as we are surrounded by places which JB knew and loved so well. Penelope and John spent all their married lives within a 20 mile radius of Oxford."

On 14th May 1994, Father John Salter, Vicar of SS Peter and Paul in Wantage, held a Mass to commemorate the tenth anniversary of John Betjeman's death. Several members of the Council of the Betjeman Society were present and Bernard & I went along as we had seen a notice in the local press. Up to that point we had no idea there was such a thing as a Betjeman Society.

Father John subsequently put another notice in the local papers saying that if there was sufficient interest, perhaps a Wantage Branch of the Betjeman Society could be formed. Again Bernard and I responded and in June 1995 we received a letter asking us to come to a meeting as Philippa Davies, Chairman and Founder of the Betjeman Society, was going to be there. She told us how she had started the Society and I can still see her perching on a stool trying to persuade us that Wantage was the obvious place for a Branch. There were about six of us present and Philippa was so enthusiastic and convincing that by the end of the evening, the Wantage Branch was born.

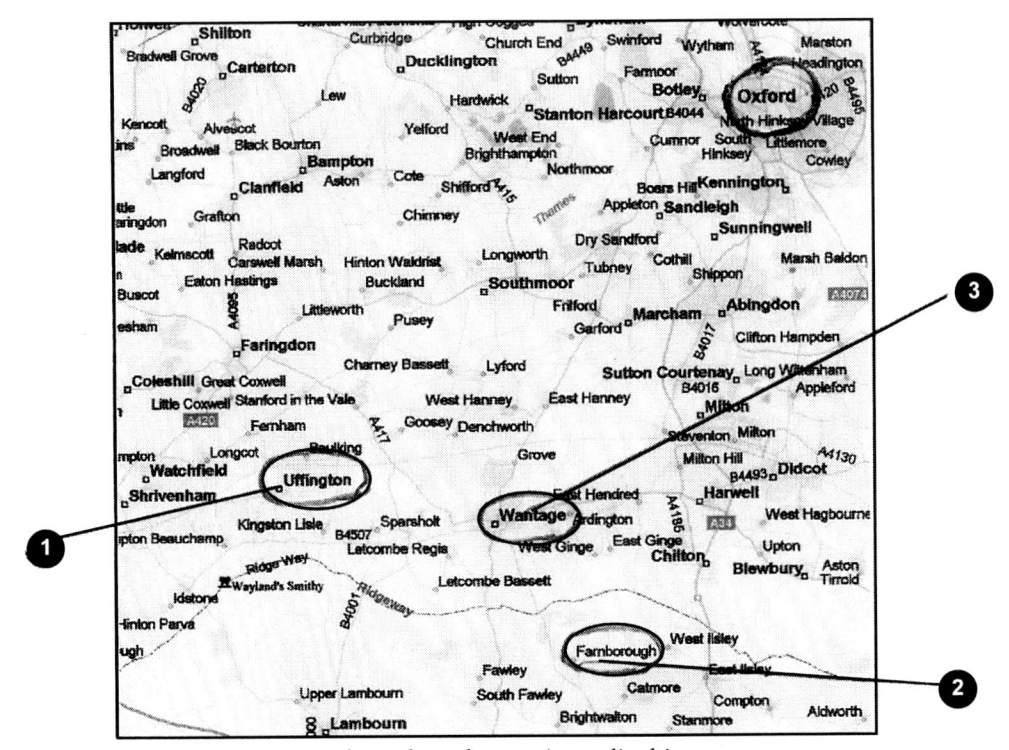

John and Penelope Betjeman lived in:
1. Garrards Farm, Uffington, 2. The Old Rectory, Farnborough and 3. The Mead, Wantage

We met again in July and in November Father John Salter arranged (and cooked) our Inaugural Dinner. The guest list comprised a few people who had expressed an interest plus Jim Moley, who was Mayor of Wantage and some members of the local Town Council. Dick and Kirsty Squires were our 'honoured guests'. Dick spoke at that dinner of the Betjemans whom he had known very well and of his travels in India with Penelope. The Squires have subsequently hosted many lunches and dinners at their home, Old Church House, in Wantage.

At this first dinner, Father John said that he was very busy and would appreciate some secretarial help. Bernard said that I could type and I became Secretary of Wantage Branch, a role which, apart from a year's sabbatical in Cornwall, I have held in one guise or another ever since. More recently, Father John has become our President, Roy Denison is our Secretary and I am Membership Secretary and Treasurer.

In January 1996, Father John, Bernard and I met to plan our meetings for the year – an AGM in March, a summer garden meeting which became 'Pimms and Poetry', a September meeting and a dinner at the end of the year.

By the end of 1996 we had built up a membership of some 30 people and since then we have tried to have at least one outing each year to a place with strong Betjeman connections. We have been to the Dragon School in Oxford and also had a very wet but extremely interesting visit to Marlborough College and saw the beautiful Chapel where JB is recorded as a famous 'old boy'.

Celebrating JB's 90th birthday at Charlton village hall, August 1996

The second annual dinner of the Wantage Branch, November 1996

Uffington was John and Penelope's first real home and at Garrards farmhouse they had stables, horses and drank milk from their own goat. On 6th January 1997, 'Twelfth Night', with kind permission of Bill and Cherry Mawle, the owners, we had a tour of the house, read *'Archie and the Strict Baptists'* by a huge log fire and had mulled wine and mince pies.

It was so comfortable it was easy to see why they had loved living there. In 1997, we were delighted to be invited by Sue and Ralph Cobham to hold our second Pimms meeting at 'The Mead'. We were told by Ralph that quite a number of improvements had been made since the Betjemans had lived there: it is no secret that Penelope's

Bernard Mattimore, Roy Burton, Father John Salter, and Pat Mattimore outside Garrards farmhouse, January 1997

Pat Mattimore, Cherry Mawle and Jose Cockrell in the kitchen at Garrards Farmhouse

priorities were not domestic. The Mead has a naturally warm and welcoming atmosphere and one felt that when the Betjemans moved there in 1951 it must have been a happy home.

It was at this second 'Pimms' meeting that Ralph Cobham unveiled plans for the proposed Betjeman Millennium Park.

To complete our visits to Betjeman homes, in July 1998 we went to the Old Rectory at Farnborough, a rather grander house on the highest point of the Berkshire Downs. We went over to the church where Michael Todhunter, now the owner of the Old Rectory, told us more about the years when JB was a Churchwarden there and we looked at the beautiful John Piper window in the church.

Philippa Davies at The Mead

In 1999 we held our 'Wantage Bells' day to commemorate 15 years since the death of JB. Father John held a Mass in the church followed by lunch at Dick and Kirsty Squires'. When Candida married in 1964, JB had presented a handwritten draft of 'Wantage Bells' to the bell ringers: it had hung in the bell tower and was starting to look a bit 'neglected'. Wantage Branch paid to have it restored and framed and it was on display in the church that day. As a 'thank you' a quarter-peal was rung and this made a wonderful accompaniment to our after-lunch stroll between 'these red brick garden walls' to look round the new Betjeman Millennium Park. We then followed the Letcombe Brook to 'The Mead' for afternoon tea. It was a truly memorable day.

In 2001 Wantage Branch was invited to host the National Society AGM and we chose to hold it at Ardington House, home of the Baring family. JB and Penelope were great friends of Dessie and Molly Baring and Paul and Candida were contemporaries and great friends of their children Peter, Nigel and Anne. It was a wonderful day

Sue Cobham clearing the ground for the Betjeman Millennium Park

and Nigel Baring was a perfect host. We had a tour of the house and grounds after lunch and were made to feel very welcome. Nigel told us that JB had said: "I have had more laughs at your house (Ardington) than I have had even at The Mead."

In 2006 we had a most interesting visit to Magdalen College, Oxford, which included an exhibition in the library of Betjeman memorabilia (specially put together for the centenary year) and Dr. David Pattison, a Fellow of Magdalen and now Chairman of the Betjeman Society and Chairman of the newly revived Oxford Branch, 'enlightened' us to the truth of the famous lines 'failed in Divinity' and some of the background to the C S Lewis feud.

Looking back over my Betjeman files, I am astonished at the number of things we have done, places we have visited, some more than once, and guests we have welcomed including Jonathan Stedall and our very special guests, Philippa and Jake Davies at our centenary dinner which again was held at Dick and Kirsty Squires' and which ended in an impromptu discussion and exchange of stories and looked like continuing into the wee small hours!

AGM at Ardington House, June 2001. Ann Heald at the back circulating the attendance book.

In 2004 Father John again held a Mass on the 20th Anniversary of JB's death and the traditional lunch was held at Dick and Kirsty Squires'. Towards the end of 2004, membership of Wantage suffered a bit of a dip and Roy & Mya Denison took the helm and asked Bernard and me if we would join them. We had just moved back from Cornwall and were very happy to do so.

Wantage is now back to its former strength and our meetings are very friendly and have a truly 'Betjeman' atmosphere - Thanks to John Salter, our President, it is a very welcoming branch and we always say "half Betjeman - half hospitality" which I feel JB would approve. We are looking ahead to 2009 and making plans to commemorate the 25th Anniversary of his death.

We have made so many friends and been to many places that the name 'John Betjeman' has opened up for us. The comment most often heard at a Betjeman event is that we feel we have been transported back to a time when life was more civilized and we are so thankful to the man and his philosophy and - most of all - his humour.

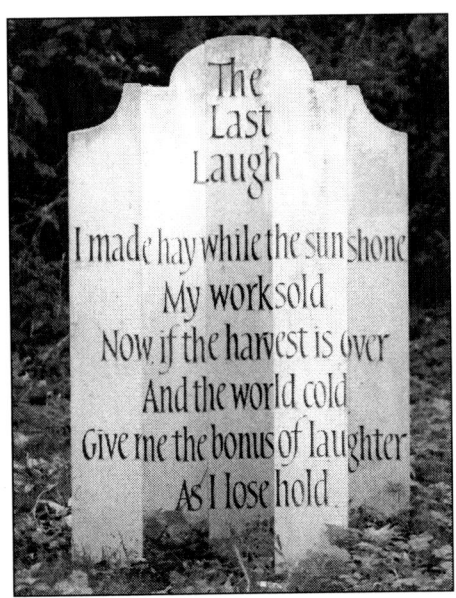

'The Last Laugh' in the Betjeman Millennium Park, Wantage

A scrapbook of the first twenty years 57

Oxford Branch

David Pattison (Chairman) writes:

The Branch was founded in 1996 by Anthony Thorn, a retired master from the Dragon School, Oxford (where JB had been a boarder from 1917-20). Several meetings were held at Anthony's home (memorable for the splendid teas provided by his wife) and branch activities then included a talk on St Barnabas' church, Oxford, excursions to Sezincote and to Uffington, a Christmas party, participation in a 'Midsummer Evensong' at Chiselhampton, and a talk by the poet and critic Jon Stallworthy.

Sadly, Anthony's health failed and in 2003 he had to stand down as organiser of the Oxford Branch. An appeal in the Society's *Newsletter* produced no volunteers to succeed him but I said that when I retired from my full-time post as university lecturer and Fellow of Magdalen College in 2005, 1 would be prepared to take on the task of reviving the Oxford Branch.

Anthony Thorn at the Dragon School in November 1996

I sent a circular to members in the area in December 2005, followed by another in April 2006, and in October that year organised a meeting to discuss our plans for the

Oxford Branch members at Sezincote, 9th September 2007

future. The first meeting of our revived branch was in December 2006 when John Ashdown, a member of the Oxford Preservation Trust with experience in local planning, gave us an illustrated talk on 'Betjeman and Oxford'.

In 2007 we held three meetings: a showing of the *Summoned by Bells* video, a visit to Sezincote and a talk from Bevis Hillier on the subject 'How to get on in Biography'.

In addition, the Society held a joint meeting in Oxford with The Philip Larkin Society at which we heard a talk from Bernard Richards, a retired member of the Oxford English faculty, on 'Betjeman and Larkin'; visits were also made to sites of interest in their lives (St John's and Magdalen Colleges, Pusey House, and Beechwood House at Iffley).

Plans for 2008 include a central Oxford walk, further showings of hard-to-find video material and talks by Leslie Mitchell, the biographer of Maurice Bowra, on 'Bowra and Betjeman' and by Hugh Compton on the Oxford Canal.

The Shires Branch

'Above the fields of Leicestershire
On arches we were born(e)...' JB

John Langford 'Liaison Man and partly PRO' writes:
Four JB zealots came together at the Oxfam cafe, Market Street, Leicester, on Tuesday 8th July 1997, with the aim of forming a Betjeman Society branch in the East Midlands. Baz Morris proved the natural Chairman; Peter James, Chancellor; the late Ken Webb, Poetry Representative and John Langford, Minister-without-Portfolio. After deliberation we decided on the name 'The Shires Branch' and our counties were: Leicester, Derby, Nottingham, Northampton, Lincoln, Rutland and the Soke of Peterborough. Lincolnshire members happily formed their own branch in October 1999.

Baz's incredible hard work - 'everybody invited' - brought 55 people to that first meeting at Leicester Adult Education College on 8th November 1997.

Over the years since then, other members joined the original committee: Dr John Florance, (a very active) President; the late Revd. Gerry Bishton - spiritual adviser, Mike Wilson - bibliophile; Horace Liberty - Betjeman books and letters; Jim Sterling - the world of films; Ann Ward - venue-fixing, catering and all-round good egg.

Gerry led three excellent tours studying Midlands churches (his obituary is in 'The Betjemanian', vol. 17, pages 58 – 60) and we hosted two Society AGMs: in Leicester in 1999 and Market Harborough in 2007.

BRANCHES: *History*

The Shires branch outside St Mary's church, Melton Mowbray
Tour leader: Revd. Gerry Bishton, Saturday 19th May 1998

Four or five meetings per year - one or two jointly with our Lincolnshire friends - has proved ideal, Baz's flamboyant flyers and 'keepsakes' becoming famous. Average attendance has been 35 - 40.

Clockwise from top left: Baz Morris, Peter James,
Ann Ward and David Weston, Horace Liberty.

60   *A scrapbook of the first twenty years*

All our events have been reported fully in the Society Newsletter. Members have also contributed to our own magazine 'Twixt the Shires' from No.1 (March 1998) to No.10 (November 2007) celebrating our 10th Anniversary. Without the energy and commitment of Baz, The Shires branch would never have taken up and maintained the profile it has. But after ten happy years, Baz and two other committee members have needed to step down.

Under our new chairman, Ann Ward, the revised committee will continue to bring the life and work of John Betjeman to delight us all in the Shire counties.

'Going places with John Betjeman' The Shires Branch, 2007

Note: Peter James, a founder member of the Shires Branch, died in May, 2008. Baz Morris remembers that when the branch was formed, Peter said:

"... it was John Betjeman who put a poetic mantle on that wisdom of hindsight to which we nearly all eventually aspire. My well-worn copy of *Summoned by Bells,* that's what did it for me. Then over the years came a greater familiarity with his poetry and I was hooked!"

Peter died after a long and brave battle against cancer. When I asked how he was he usually replied: "Not too bad!" He was a dear friend who will be sadly missed. Not too bad? I think he was in fact absolutely great! (BM)

Isle of Man Branch

Joyce Corlett (Secretary/Treasurer) writes:

The Isle of Man Branch of the Betjeman Society was officially launched on 20th June 1999 by Prunella Scales and Timothy West who were at that time taking part in the annual Mananan Festival.

The first business meeting was held on 11th September that year and was attended by 13 members. The first Chairman was His Honour Deemster Arthur Luft who drew up our Constitution. It was approved at the Meeting held on 2nd October 1999 at the home of our first Vice-Chairman, Mr. Timothy Atkinson and his wife, Angela.

Since that time, an average of four meetings a year have taken place. One of these meetings is always held on the Sunday nearest to JB's birthday and takes the form of a picnic or birthday party depending on the weather.

In September 2001, Mr John Bethell, a Founder Member and current Chairman of the Erin Arts Centre, and a man who knew JB well, became

20th June 1999: official launch of the Isle of Man Branch at the Erin Arts Centre left to right: Betty Beale, Eunice Salmond, John Bethel, Dorothy and Arthur Luft, with Prunella Scales

Chairman of the I.O.M. Branch of the Betjeman Society. As John Bethell and Joyce Corlett were also Chairman and Secretary of the Erin Arts Centre it became possible for the Betjeman Society to make good use of the Erin Arts Centre literary events: these have included a performance by Tim Heath of 'Summoned by Bells', a visit of the Poet Laureate, Andrew Motion, and Robert Daws' presentation of 'Summoned by Betjeman'.

Mrs. Sally Macfadyen, wife of His Excellency the Lieutenant Governor, was a member of our branch in 2005, when 14 members of various other U.K. branches visited the

Island. A highlight of that visit was an invitation to visit Government House, where we were shown round the grounds before being served afternoon tea. The following day the visiting members attended the I.O.M. Branch's A.G.M. and buffet lunch; the guest speaker was Philippa Davies.

In 2006 we celebrated Betjeman's centenary with a special service at Old Ballaugh Church. This was recorded and later broadcast by Manx Radio. Also, in the centenary year, 'Isle of Man Post' in conjunction with the National Portrait Gallery issued a set of eight stamps featuring portraits of people who had links with the island. JB's portrait by Stephen Hyde featured on the 64p stamp.

The Betjeman stamp issued by 'Isle of Man Post' in 2006

And so we continue in our own small way. We have only 13 members at present but we have recently provided a plaque within the Erin Arts Centre which has been fixed in what is now a dedicated 'Betjeman Centenary Foyer' as a constant reminder of a great man and a talking point for all visitors.

Dedication of the plaque in the Erin Arts centre. l to r: Joyce Corlett, John Bethel and John Bowring (archivist).

Lincolnshire Branch

Michael Thomas (Chairman) wrote:

Wishing to start a branch, I had persuaded a local newspaper to make an announcement that a meeting would be held in Louth on Saturday, 23rd October 1999. Twenty interested people turned up to our inaugural meeting.

It was decided that the branch would be run on an informal basis with a 'pay as you go' policy, and that I should act as Chairman. We didn't attract anyone from Louth to join our ranks so when Stuart Crooks (Director of the Lincolnshire Wildlife Trust) offered the use of their H.Q. at Banovallum House in Horncastle, we gratefully accepted as it is a lovely Georgian house, centrally situated in the county.

On average, we attract 15 to 20 members to our meetings. It soon became clear that there was a preference for a mixture of discussion meetings and outdoor events. The latter have been very successful and, in conjunction with The Shires Branch, we have had some interesting visits: exploring the Roman town of Horncastle, the Edwardian Woodhall Spa and Kings Lynn, all places that Betjeman himself admired. We claim to be the only Branch, to date, to share its activities with another one.

Kit Lawie, using her artistic skills, produced a Betjeman Society calendar in 2001, raising over £100 for the Parkinson's Society. The calendar is a first, and book collectors are missing something if they haven't got one!

By 2003 we were in a position to offer ourselves as hosts to the rest of the Betjeman Society and, with welcome input from the Shires Branch, the AGM was held on 7th June at The Lawn, Lincoln. Many of our visitors had never been there before and we were able to show them some of its glories.

Our members, being keen Betjemanians, soon discovered that our hero paid many visits to the county. We found people who remembered JB and in 2006 the results of our research and their memories were put into a book to celebrate Betjeman's centenary year. This was published as *Betjeman's Lincolnshire*. The print run of 1,000 copies was sold out within six months of its publication and we were able to donate £500 to the Lincolnshire Old Churches Trust.

The 'book launch' was a wonderful event held in Sausthorpe Old Hall. It was attended by more than fifty Society members.

The Betjeman Society calendar for 2002 by Kit Lawie

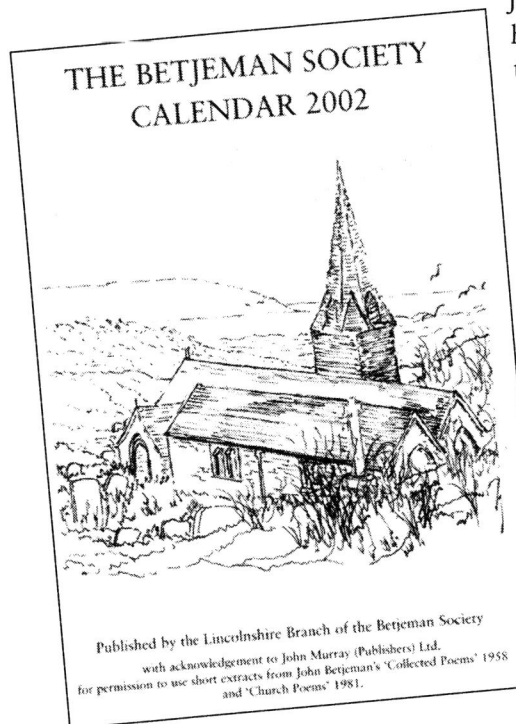

John Betjeman himself stayed at the Old Hall forty years ago and we were able to invite Margaret Ward, who worked there at that time, to tell us about her memories of meeting JB and talking to him about Lincolnshire dialect.

Following in JB's footsteps we have also organised 'church crawls'. A very interesting one, led by the Revd. Cliff Knowles, started at Brant Broughton (shown on the front cover of our book) and ended at Belton (home of Peggy Purey-Cust's ancestors) with its magnificent collection of memorials, arguably the best in any English parish church. This visit was also supported by the Shires Branch.

'Betjeman's Lincolnshire' was published in 2006

In an earlier church crawl we were pleased to find the grave of Theophilus Caleb and his wife under the snowdrops in Huttoft churchyard. He was the Indian priest in Betjeman's poem *A Lincolnshire Church*.

Looking ahead, we hope to make further discoveries about JB's incursions into Lincolnshire and to

The churchyard and 'slanting' gravestones at Huttoft

bring together more people who share our pleasure in his works.

Note: Michael Thomas died shortly after writing this report. He will be sadly missed.

Michael Thomas with the 'Shell Guide to Lincolnshire' in Westgate, Louth 2006

Ridings Branch
Peter Scott writes:
Shirley Hughes-Rowlands started the whole thing off with a "call to arms" letter to members in the North, on 20th April 2008. Derek Clarkson took up the baton and wrote to the 12 respondents on 4th July. The replies to that letter led to his being able to arrange the first meeting in Harrogate on Thursday 25th September. Nine people attended, and it was there that the name of the Ridings Branch was adopted. John Langford (Shires Branch) came to "push us in the right direction". We agreed to meet again on Thursday 13th November, and six of the nine duly did so. The third gathering is now set for Thursday 8th January 2009. The centre of gravity of the Branch certainly seems to be Harrogate.

In the August Newsletter, John Heald states that editing a Newsletter "is less dangerous than putting up a shelf". Derek Clarkson will be able to second that, because he was hanging up a shower curtain, fell and broke his leg - which is why he was absent in November!

Bygone Branches
Birmingham
Jo Hunt was the founder and driving force behind the Birmingham Branch. At the grand launch in 1991 at the Birmingham and Midland Institute he invited the well-known poet Edward Lowbury and lecturer Anthony Morton to address the meeting. Jo was a good source of information and ideas. He introduced us to The Alliance of Literary Societies and encouraged us to devise a system whereby we could contact our members county by county. The Midlands was the first area to be grouped for mail shots. Traditionally the Branch held four meetings per year until ill health prevented Jo from continuing.

Ireland
For some time George Peche was the only member in Ireland and in 1994 he hosted a visit to Betjeman-related places in his homeland. This hugely successful event enjoyed by six members of the Society led to a letter being published in The Irish Times and in 1995 he founded a Branch. Eventually he gathered five members and they met twice a year in George's flat in Dublin. George will also be remembered for his whistle-stop tour of the *Lost Villages of Heathrow*. These were all familiar to him from his days of working as a journalist.

Oxford University
Edward Wild saw a short note about the founding of the Betjeman Society in The Times when he was in the 6th form at Sedbergh. He joined immediately, spoke on Betjeman whilst still at school and continued his support when he went up to Keble. Once there, he founded the Oxford University Branch. Luckily he kept some records. An inaugural dinner was held on 13th February 1992 at Michael's Restaurant with Humphrey Carpenter as their special guest. From that launch they went on to invite many well-known speakers such as Bill Deedes, Auberon Waugh, Professor Martin Stannard, Patrick Taylor Martin and Bevis Hillier. Sundry diary stories in the national

press resulted, " the most reassuring news I have heard from that quarter for some time" said Auberon Waugh in the Literary Review. Blackwell's sponsored a Betjeman Memorial prize. The events card they produced was possibly the model for the one currently issued by the Society. Their membership grew to 100. Undergradates were elected to serve one term as President and names on the list after Edward are Michael Ffinch, Samuel Robinson, Dan Stacey and James Anderson. Where are they now? Edward is in touch with us.

Bristol and later Weston-Super-Mare

We first met Bill Pickard when he came to the picnic in St Enodoc churchyard in 1989. On that occasion he brought a magnificent cake and it established our tradition of having a birthday cake at our Society's annual party. Already involved in literary circles (the title he used for his groups was Circle in the Square) he went on to found and run these two Branches. Bill always insisted that there should be no alcohol or anyone under 18 at his meetings. As a statistician he estimates that he has hosted 70 house groups and meetings, three major public meetings with the Society's travelling exhibition and more than 1000 people have been seen at his Betjeman events. He has been our resident poet and a regular correspondent, his envelopes always stuck securely with the strongest sellotape known to man. On retirement first from the church then from voluntary roles, he recently published another book, his biography, which he has called Memoir out of the Ordinary, Poet Luck.

On the steps of the Congregational Church, Market Harborough

AGM at Market Harborough. Anna Gammond, John Florance and Ellen Richardson

EVENTS: *Gallery*

THE DAILY TELEGRAPH,
1998

DINNERS

The Betjeman Society
Lady Wilson of Rievaulx presided and read from an unpublished poem at the 10th anniversary dinner of The Betjeman Society held on Saturday at Butchers' Hall. Mr Peter Gammond, Chairman, and Mrs Philippa Davies, Vice-Chairman, welcomed members and their guests. Mrs Candida Lycett Green, Mr Bevis Hillier and Mr John Heald also spoke.

Horace Liberty, Reg Eden, David Pattison as new Chairman, and Bevis Hillier at 2008 AGM.

10th Anniversary party of the Canterbury Branch

John and Triss Cottenden with Candida Lycett Green in Uffington, 1997

THE DAILY TELEGRAPH,
September 11th 2006

Dinners

The Betjeman Society
The Betjeman Society held its 2006 Centenary Dinner on Saturday at Butchers' Hall, to celebrate the 100th anniversary year of the birth of Sir John Betjeman. The speakers were Mr Peter Gammond, Mr Kenneth Pinnock, Mrs Philippa Davies, Mr Edward Mirzoeff and Mr John Heald.

THE TIMES, 1998

Dinners

Betjeman Society
Lady Wilson of Rievaulx presided and read an unpublished poem by John Betjeman at a dinner to mark the 10th anniversary of the Betjeman Society held on Saturday at Butchers' Hall. Mr Peter Gammond, chairman, and Mrs Philippa Davies, vice-chairman, welcomed the guests. Mrs Candida Lycett Green, Mr Bevis Hillier and Mr John Heald also spoke.

Ken Pinnock speaking to Society members about Cathedral water cisterns on Bookfair Day, May 2008

68 *A scrapbook of the first twenty years*

EVENTS: *Red Letter Days*

MARLBOROUGH, 1990
Joan Hunter Dunn tennis tournament and Society weekend

Philippa Davies

With strains of *A Subaltern's Lovesong* ringing in our ears we gathered on the playing fields of Marlborough College to take part in the Joan Hunter Dunn tennis tournament. We played before tea and after tea, he against she, in random pairings of doubles until winners emerged.

"And cool the veranda that welcomed us in, to the six-o-clock news and a lime juice and gin."

Refreshed and rested, the players and all the spectators participated in the prize giving and dinner at the Ivy House in the High Street of Marlborough. Slazenger kindly sponsored us and gave the tennis balls and most generously gave rackets for the winners. However, the prize that every player will most treasure is the certificate they each received, signed by Joan Hunter Dunn in her distinctive hand.

Joanna Jackson née Hunter Dunn taken from the Order of Service for her funeral on 2nd May 2008

It was also a novel experience to find ourselves being interviewed for a newspaper. Colin Dunn of *The Mail on Sunday* produced a four page spread of photographs and text which duly appeared in all its glory in the 'You' magazine of 19th August 1990. That, too, has become a collectors' item.

Sunday was another fine day and we joined Terry Rogers, the College Archivist of Marlborough College for a tour of classrooms, the site of 'Big Fire', the dormitories, the portrait by JB's aunt, the so called in-houses and out-houses, the mound, the shell grotto, the cricket pitches and, of course, the chapel. Ranged in the pews facing

A scrapbook of the first twenty years 69

EVENTS: *Red Letter Days*

Robert, Lucy and Emily Shaw, Anthony Stern, William and Jake Davies at the Joan Hunter Dunn tennis tournament, Marlborough, 1990

Philippa Davies and Mike Read: the tournament winners

Bill Pickard: "We don't want people to think we're eccentrics"

one another we could swing our minds back across the years to the early 1900s when 'the athletes' would have faced 'the aesthetes'.

Joanna Jackson, née Hunter Dunn, was one of the world's truly unstated people. Anyone who met her felt better for the encounter. Many times she had expressed similar sentiments about JB. He showed kindness beyond all imagination to 'Joan' and her children when she lost her husband at a young age.

The Society was highly honoured when our then Chairman, John Heald, was invited by her three sons to read 'A Subaltern's Love Song' at her funeral service on 2nd May 2008.

70 *A scrapbook of the first twenty years*

WESTMINSTER ABBEY, 1998
JB's memorial dedication

Philippa Davies

The memorial to Sir John Betjeman in Poets' Corner was unveiled on 11th November 1998. It was the climax of years of careful negotiations and gentle regular reminders to The Very Reverend Michael Mayne, Dean of Westminster Abbey, reinforcing the fact that the popularity of our late Poet Laureate was lasting. The largest and perhaps the most telling part we were able to play was to prove it, by showing him the increasing numbers of members in the Society. Betjeman's popularity was as strong if not stronger than ever.

The Abbey's unofficial rule is that any contender for a memorial in Poets' Corner must have been dead at least ten years. This we accepted and 14 years after his death our patience paid off.

On our first visit, the Dean showed us an area of floor which had been selected as suitable. Unfortunately, that day, chairs were covering at least part of the area. We pointed that out as the reason for our hesitation for unqualified acceptance, i.e. polite refusal. We held our breath and waited another year or two. By then their plans had changed and in order to fit more names into Poets' Corner the Dean decided to engrave them in the windows of the South Transept. These were high, well above eye level, and dependent on good light. Again we expressed hesitation.

The next visit was a case of third offer lucky. A beautiful stone cartouche had been found by Tony Platt, Keeper of the Lapidarium, in store in the triforium and as soon as it was ascertained that there was no other call for it we were asked to submit some favourite quotations. Simplicity won the day: no quotes, just name and dates and so JB's wishes were complied with too.

The stone was sent to York to be cut. Donald Buttress, the Abbey's Keeper of the Fabric, arranged the repairs and mounting of the cartouche. David Peace drew the lettering, complete with the finest

Tony Platt, the keeper of Lapidarium at Westminster Abbey, beside JB's Cartouche, 2004

EVENTS: *Red Letter Days*

flourishes, and set the cartouche on a small stone plinth of carved prayer books.

At the dedication service Mary Lady Wilson of Rievaulx was invited to unveil the memorial, and flowers were placed by Candida Lycett Green's grandchildren.

Joanna Lumley read some of JB's poetry and Patrick Leigh Fermor gave a splendid address. The Dean, the Reverend Michael Mayne, presided.

This very special day was rounded off at the nearby Vitello D'Oro restaurant with a reception for the Society's members and their invited guests, Vice Presidents and our President, Lady Wilson.

(Picture by kind permission of Picture Partnership)

Candida Lycett Green and her grandchildren, Jasmine and Archie Ward

(Picture by kind permission of Picture Partnership)

Patrick Leigh Fermor gave the address at the dedication service

72 *A scrapbook of the first twenty years*

2006 The Centenary Year – 365 Red Letter days!

Martin Revill

My wife, Margaret, and I joined the Society in 1998 shortly after the unveiling and dedication of the Memorial to Sir John in Poets' Corner in Westminster Abbey. Looking back over the many varied and fascinating events of the Society during its first 10 years, we felt that we had surely missed so much. Over the past ten years since our joining however the programme of activities has continued and maintained the consistently high standard of fun and education.

It is perhaps a little far-fetched to claim 365 red letter days in that year (and we each have our favourites). There was so much going on – not only in the Society but in the country generally. The press coverage was great and did boost the membership of the Society.

Planning activities for the Society for the 2006 Centenary Year started two years earlier when a sub-committee was formed comprising John Cottenden, Michael Wilson and myself for this purpose. The job proved to be mostly great fun, a little frustrating at times, but very satisfying at the end of the year. John Heald, in his Chairman's Letter, stated at the beginning of the year: " The indefatigable Candida has arranged an enormous and most varied programme in memory of her father and in aid of charities associated with him. Radio and television companies have been busy ransacking their archives and preparing new films and broadcasts to mark his birthday. There will be books, newspaper articles and exhibitions galore. Finally, Sir John, or perhaps I should say plaques bearing his name, will be unveiled more frequently than Salome ever was."

It would take another book to recall all that went on that year but a taster recalls – the Oxford coach tour - Betjeman's Oxford; the publication, by the Lincolnshire branch, of that wonderful book *Betjeman's Lincolnshire;* plaques unveiled at Garrards' Farm, 31 Highgate, and St. Anne's Church Highgate; and of course the superb Gala Performance at the Prince of Wales Theatre in London – an event graced with the attendance of HRH The Prince of Wales and HRH The Duchess of Cornwall – at which a galaxy of stars performed hosted by one of our Vice-Presidents, Barry Humphries CBE; and finally the publication by our Vice-Chairman Peter Gammond of his *Little Book of Betjeman*. What a year!

One of the highlights of the year was a ceremony at Westminster Abbey. John Cottenden reported: "Following a welcome from the Sub-Dean, Canon Robert Wright conducted the short service of prayers with a reading from St. Paul. We listened to Bevis Hillier, JB's official biographer, recount his memories of Sir John. He was followed by Mary

EVENTS: *Red Letter Days*

Lady Wilson of Rievaulx, the Society's President, who laid a posy of white roses at the foot of the memorial cartouche to Sir John. To complete the ceremony, the Society's Chairman, John Heald read an extract from 'Coming Home', a 1943 BBC broadcast by JB.

"The service ended with prayers and a final blessing from the Sub-Dean."

Left: Candida Lycett Green and Paul Betjeman at the train naming ceremony, Liverpool Street Station. 8th September 2006.

Below: Dinner at Butcher's Hall 2006

(Picture by kind permission of Margaret Revill)

For me, two events stand out in that year.

Firstly, the weekend of 9-10 September – The Centenary Dinner at Butchers' Hall, London, and the Gala Performance (mentioned above). This was to be the last event John Cottenden attended.

Philippa and Jake Davies had rented the flat at 43 Cloth Fair, a home of John Betjeman himself, from the Landmark Trust for the whole weekend and a number of members accepted their kind invitation to visit them there before the Dinner which was held just around the corner. A door off the side alley gave access to a narrow twisting staircase which led up to the first floor landing and two rooms. The drawing room was 14ft square with William Morris wallpaper and stuffed with Betjeman books. A further staircase led up to a bedroom and bathroom. The flat has a view across to the church of St. Bartholomew the Great and is situated above *Betjeman's Winebar*, itself the venue for the first Society dinner. A photograph was taken inside the flat to commemorate our visit.

On arrival at Butchers' Hall members and their guests gathered in the lobby before moving on to a reception room where drinks were served. An air of excitement and expectation prevailed. We ascended the grand staircase to the splendid dining room. Our President, Lady Mary Wilson looked resplendent in a royal blue flowing gown. Philippa had arranged 100 longiflorum lilies in tall blue vases which alternated with the candelabra on the long banqueting tables. Members enjoyed a sumptuous feast. The toast to the guests was proposed by Peter Gammond and responded to by Kenneth Pinnock. This was followed by the toast to Sir John, proposed by Philippa Davies and responded to by Edward Mirzeoff. John Heald proposed a toast to The Betjeman Society and finally a most enjoyable evening was rounded off with Betty Beale proposing the Society toast "The Bonus of Laughter".

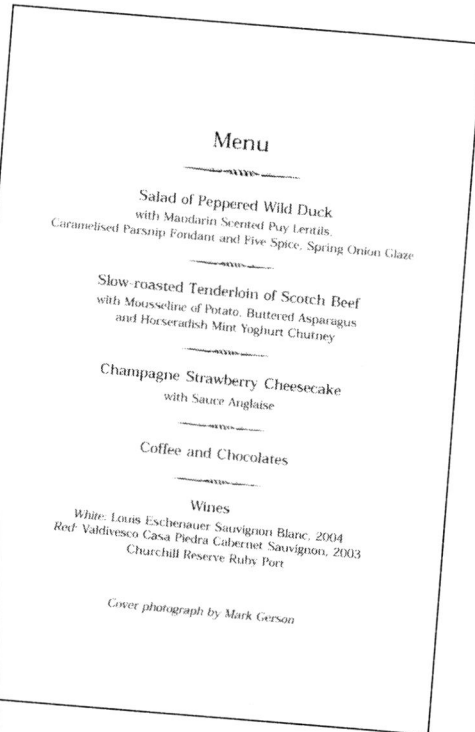

Philippa Davies, Michael and Elizabeth Thomas, John Langford and Ann Ward at 43 Cloth Fair.

(Picture by kind permission of Margaret Revill)

THE BETJEMAN SOCIETY

1906-2006
Sir John Betjeman

THE CENTENARY DINNER

Butchers' Hall · City of London
Saturday, 9th September 2006

Menu

Salad of Peppered Wild Duck
with Mandarin Scented Puy Lentils,
Caramelised Parsnip Fondant and Five Spice, Spring Onion Glaze

Slow-roasted Tenderloin of Scotch Beef
with Mousseline of Potato, Buttered Asparagus
and Horseradish Mint Yoghurt Chutney

Champagne Strawberry Cheesecake
with Sauce Anglaise

Coffee and Chocolates

Wines
White: Louis Eschenauer Sauvignon Blanc, 2004
Red: Valdivesco Casa Piedra Cabernet Sauvignon, 2003
Churchill Reserve Ruby Port

Cover photograph by Mark Gerson

As a former railwayman myself, the second event that stands out for me was the weekend in York which took place at the end of September. Unfortunately John Cottenden was by that time too unwell to join the event which he had done so much to help organize.

John Langford wrote: "Society members travelled from far and wide to make up a splendid attendance at the National Railway Museum at York. Before lunch many visited the two great museum halls depicting railway history and heritage. John Heald was pleased to introduce our speaker Richard Hardy, a long-term career railway man, writer on the subject and friend of John Betjeman. He outlined his own varied career after leaving Marlborough, alluding to his practical training and 'the great brotherhood of railwaymen'. On first meeting JB he realised how he loved railway people – from chauffeur to secretary to station master – 'making them feel ten feet tall'. Later in his career, Mr. Hardy was able to invite JB onto Saloon tours over parts of the railway network under his jurisdiction. 'This is my Victorian drawing room', said JB on first entering an old GNR Saloon for a run to Peterborough.

"John Heald then introduced Alan Wilmott, a well-known name in the world of British Transport Films, who showed us a number of films, or extracts, in which JB either appeared or narrated.

(Picture by kind permission of Margaret Revill)

Richard Hardy signing a book for Martin Revill

"Our venue for Saturday evening was Bedern Hall in York, one of the medieval halls of the city, and home of three ancient Guilds. After a splendid meal provided by the resident caterers 'Time and Place', members listened to some poetry with a railway setting from John Langford and Ann Ward and heard from Roy Denison of JB's love for the Great Western.

"On Sunday morning members assembled at the Castle steps in the City to be taken on a fascinating walking tour led by Darrell Buttery, Chairman of the York Civic Trust. Our guide showed us many of the City's fine medieval Guild Halls tucked away in small side streets and spoke of the conflict between planners seeking to erect new residential blocks and the need to preserve the spirit – and vistas – of such an ancient city. Beside the Minster, a delightful enclave happily free of road traffic, our guide quoted some of JB's words from a visit in 1964:

"'Take me to the Horace Field Building', ('that baroque "Palace of Business", the HQ of the North Eastern Railway, by the NER architect William Bell with detailing by Horace Field'. JB concluded, after his tour: 'One of the best days I can recall in a long life: sun on grass and stone and brick – and gin in the William IV.'"

ST PANCRAS, 2007
The Greatest Cathedral of Them All -
Some random thoughts about the new St Pancras

John Langford

*Sculpture of Sir John Betjeman by Martin Jennings
unveiled at St Pancras Station on 12th November 2007*

(Photograph courtesy of Clifford Knowles)

Mercifully, no-one asked me to nominate my most precious Betjeman moment of Centenary Year 2006. The whole calendar provided such a box of delights that declaring a choice would indeed be invidious. But undoubtedly for me the red letter day of the year 2007 was first encountering the new St Pancras - on the afternoon of its public opening to Eurostar continental trains on Wednesday 14th November.

Arriving later in the day, I had not witnessed the orchestra playing Elgar which had accompanied the very first Eurostar train (a VIP special) departing at 11 o'clock. (In Victorian times the favourite for such occasions was 'See the Conquering Hero Comes'). Nor had I mingled with the mighty at the actual unveiling of the statue of Sir John

Betjeman by Martin Jennings, which had taken place before an invited audience on Monday 12th November. But, for us, the greatest enduring joy is that everyone - just everyone, Betjemanian or no - loves the statue.

They know why JB is there and tell their friends to beat a path to St Pancras. People even stop to read the extracts from Betjeman poems, chosen by Martin Jennings, in the roundels set in the station concourse. Society members were given space in *The Betjemanian,* vol. 19, pages 33 to 37, to wax lyrical over the restoration of the station roof, and indeed over the statue, so those remarks will not be repeated here. The whole station restoration is, of course, a tremendous triumph for Victorian railway architecture, for trains - both continental and 'domestic' ('BR' to you and me!), as well as for our hero, John Betjeman.

But on opening night, or rather evening, of the Eurostar service, after giving Sir John a hearty handshake, I was happy to saunter off to The Baby Betjeman bar and settle down to contemplate - over a decent glass of red. Out on the concourse, just by the Eurostar buffer stops, was a small table for three, one seat occupied by a well-set chap in tweeds with a long beard and well into a large whisky (or possibly whiskey). To hand, a nice little water jug in bone china. He'll do, I thought. Falling into conversation over the happy occasion and, of course, Betjeman, my new friend soon introduced me to no less a person than the architect (of the whole thing), Alastair Lansley. On accepting my impromptu congratulations on behalf of The Betjeman Society and hearing my request that he consider addressing us at some stage, he soon proffered his card and we parted with hearty good wishes in both directions. What a scoop!

In the months since the opening (these notes are being put together in October 2008), the level beneath the platforms, called 'the undercroft', has become one huge shopping mall (or 'maul'), where you can eat and drink and purchase pricey things all day long. More wisely, though, study those Midland Railway cast-iron pillars supporting what is above: they are said to be set exactly three Burton beer barrels apart. Bass (that's draught beer) rested here before going out all round the London streets by horse and dray. (A mechanical hoist at the platform end lowered the wagons of beer down to this level).

Love it or loathe it, all this industry below does draw the crowds to St Pancras, but a result is that parts of the concourse at platform level can be surprisingly quiet, even at busy periods. This may alter of course, when the hotel takes on its full role.
Not everyone likes it, but you should not miss Paul Day's 30ft sculpture at the hotel end of the concourse, depicting a French woman reunited with her English lover and modelled on the artist and his Gallic wife.

Reverting to drink for a moment, I don't think you can get a pint of Bass at St Pancras station today (though, of course, menus do change), but a very satisfactory alternative at The Betjeman Arms (as The Baby Betjeman has become) is 'Doom Bar', a draught beer brewed in Cornwall by Sharp's at the village of Rock, just across the ferry from Padstow.

More Betjemanian than beer, of course, might be a glass of bubbly at the longest champagne bar in the western world. (95.8 metres). I wouldn't know: I don't drink the stuff!'

Some quoteable quotes:

St Pancras was a fourteen-year-old Christian boy, who was martyred in Rome in AD 304 by the Emperor Diocletian. - JB

From today, 14th November 2007, every Eurostar journey will be carbon neutral at no extra cost to the traveller. - Eurostar's opening day booklet.

It was great to be there – even without a train to catch. - Sharon Griffiths, Eastern Daily Press.

Outcry over (the loss of) the Doric Arch probably saved St Pancras. - Rail News, February 2008.

Hurrah for Sir John Betjeman (who was) determined to save what he called 'a cathedral of commerce'. - Joan Collins, Eastern Daily Press Saturday Magazine.

A Midland Railway poster of St Pancras as it was in 1868 extolling the company's route to London and its terminus

St Pancras International in 2007

Martin Jennings, sculptor of JB, in his studio in Oxford May 2008

EVENTS OF THE BETJEMAN SOCIETY
1987 to 2008

Date	Event	Place	Particulars
1987			
07/10/87	First House Group meeting by invitation	The Davies' house, Haleswood, Canterbury	The first local meeting with 10 people present. Poems by Betjeman were read. The suggestion was made that we write to Murray's, JB's publisher, and ask to be introduced to other similar Betjeman groups.
1988			
02/03/88	Second House Group meeting	The Lissaman's, Oldway House, Fordwich	More Betjeman poems plus passages of prose were read. Other poets were introduced. Eleven people present. Letters of encouragement from Jock Murray, Lady Elizabeth Cavendish and Candida Lycett Green had been received. Jock Murray knew of no other similar groups. The possibility of a memorial stone in Poets' Corner was discussed. John Lissaman became auditor.
21/11/88	First Open Meeting	The Old Synagogue, King's School, Canterbury	Professor Mike Irwin was the speaker who chose the title *Toothbrush, Tram and Tennis Racket*. Volunteers came forward to serve on a founder committee. A collection after the talk realised £17.55.
1989			
14/03/89	Do It Yourself poetry reading	The Old Synagogue, Canterbury	Return visit to the Old Synagogue, for a reading of poems by JB and a selection of parodies.
07/06/89	First London Dinner	Betjeman's Wine Bar, 43 Cloth Fair, City of London	First meeting away from Canterbury. The Lord Mayor of London and Prunella Scales performed the unveiling of the Blue Plaque to JB at 43 Cloth Fair. Dinner was held at Betjeman's Wine Bar in the evening.
06/09/89	First Birthday Lecture	Waterstone's, Hampstead, London	Bevis Hillier launched the paperback of his book *Young Betjeman* and gave a sneak preview of Volume Two. Jock and Diana Murray were present. Large audience due to mention in *Hampstead and Highgate Express* by the editor.
26/09/89	Talk	The Old Synagogue, Canterbury	A talk on architecture and *A Betjeman view of Canterbury: Preservation or Bust* by Mansell Jagger, Director of Planning, Canterbury City Council.
22/10/89	Canterbury Literary Festival Performance	St Alphege Centre, Canterbury	*Playcraft* selected and performed *Sand in the Sandwiches, Betjeman by the Sea* for the Canterbury Festival, our first contribution to a literary festival (JB was patron of the St Alphege Centre). A huge home-made tea was served.
16/12/89	Tea Dance	Waldorf Hotel, London	Tea and dancing were combined with readings by Fiona Pitt Kethley and interviews by Val Hennessy of the *Daily Mail*.

DATE	EVENT	PLACE	PARTICULARS
1990			
31/01/90	D.I.Y. Poetry Reading	The Old Synagogue, Canterbury	A variety of poems by JB and many others were read and sung. Some people read their own compositions.
12/02/90	Talk	The Voice Box, Poetry Library, Royal Festival Hall, London	Pennie Denton presented *Betjeman's Vision of Britain*, followed by a reception.
02/03/90	Inauguration of the Canterbury Branch	Cavendish House, Canterbury	Poetry Reading at the home of Robert LLoyd, first chairman of the Canterbury Branch and cousin of Peggy Purey-Cust.
28/03/90	Performance	Burgh House, Hampstead, London	Solo performance of *Summoned by Bells* by Tim Heath who was wearing JB's dinner jacket.
05/05/90	First AGM	Dominican Priory, Canterbury	Chairman Dr James "Jim" Gibson. Despite an alarming smell of gas we escaped any great drama and shared a grand tea. A tour of the Cathedral followed.
07/08/90	Society Weekend	Marlborough town and College	Joan Hunter Dunn Tennis Tournament, lime juice and gin at 6 o'clock, dinner and prize-giving at the Ivy House. Sunday tour of Marlborough College led by Terry Rogers.
08/09/90	Walk and picnic	Highgate, London	Led by Robert Shaw from Brookfield Mansions up West Hill to a picnic in Mr Donald Barron's garden, Fitzroy Park.
14/09/90	Second Birthday Lecture	St Saviour's, Highbury, London	Jim Gibson spoke on *Thomas Hardy, John Betjeman and Twentieth Century Poetry*. The Florence Trust, formed as a studio for many artists, welcomed us even though it was still in its early stages, as was the restoration of the church.
12/11/90	Film and talk	CFS Studio, Portman Close, London	Eddie Mirzoeff and the team who directed and filmed *Metroland* shared their high and low points and amusing moments before showing the film.
1991			
31/01/91	Talk	The Old Synagogue, Canterbury	Henry Claridge of the English Department at University of Kent chose the title *The Poets Laureate*.
06/04/91	Visit and walk	City of London	View of several churches: St Bart's the Less and Great, St Anne, St Botolph, St Vedast and ending with Tim Heath in the crypt of St Paul's. The day was skilfully rescued by Tim Heath after we heard of the death of our guide, Lawrence Jones.
11/05/91	Second AGM	The Dominican Priory, Canterbury	Chairman Jim Gibson. A tea dance followed with music provided by Doug Inkpen.
02/06/91	Visit	Oxford and Oxfordshire	Visit to Magdalen College and chapel. An afternoon visit to Sezincote was hosted by the owner, Mrs Tessa Peake.
25/09/91	Inauguration of the Birmingham Branch	Birmingham and Midland Institute	Hosted by Chairman of the Birmingham Branch, Jo Hunt, the Institute's administrator. Edward Lowbury introduced the evening and Anthony Morton recited.
20/10/91	Third Birthday Lecture	The Old Synagogue, Canterbury	Dr Tim Hands presented *Summoned by What? Betjeman's Response to the Poet's Calling*. A birthday cake and tea were served.

EVENTS: Diary 1987-2008

DATE	EVENT	PLACE	PARTICULARS
22/11/91	Joint meeting	Royal Entomological Society, Queens Gate, London	Combined meeting with the Victorian Society. A selection of Victorian prose and poetry: *Betjeman: Illustrated in a Series of Picturesque Views* - a talk by Dr Andrew Sanders, lecturer in English Literature, London University.

1992

DATE	EVENT	PLACE	PARTICULARS
30/01/92	Talk	The Old Synagogue, Canterbury	Dr Christopher Taylor, Lecturer in Politics, University of Kent, *The Poetry of Churches*.
20/03/92	Talk	St Paul's Girls School, London	Jim Parker of the Barrow Poets told the story of setting JB's poems to music.
17/05/92	Third AGM	Murray's, 50 Albemarle Street, Piccadilly, London	Reminiscences by President Jock Murray and Hon Sec Ken Pinnock of life and times and even work at Murray's. Philippa Davies was elected Chairman in succession to Jim Gibson. Tea was taken at The Royal Overseas League. Later some members took a ride on a steam train from Harrow to Amersham.
11/07/92	Coach tour	Metroland, North London	*Metroland Meander from Baker Street to Verney Junction and back.* Visits included Grim's Dyke and Len Rawle and the enormous organ in his house. Devised and led by Ted Griffin.
25-27/9/92	Society weekend and Fourth Birthday Lecture	Trebetherick	Visit to Manor Farm, Huish, to Candida Lycett Green's library of Betjeman. Birthday talk by Mervyn, Lord Horder and dinner at The John Betjeman Centre, Wadebridge. Mervyn kindly stepped in at short notice due to illness of Dr Kinsman Barker. Golf competition for The Hon Sec's Golf Trophy and evensong at St Enodoc.
23/10/92	Recital and performance	University of Surrey, Guildford	*Pot Pourri in a Surrey Institute* devised and performed by students of the University.
29/11/92	Visit	St James' Palace, London	Organised and introduced by Robert Shaw. Guided by staff of the Palace and followed by tea at St James' Church, Piccadilly.

1993

DATE	EVENT	PLACE	PARTICULARS
26/02/93	Talk	The Old Synagogue Canterbury	Canon Derek Ingram Hill, the greatest authority at the time on Canterbury Cathedral, spoke on *How Betjeman Taught us to Enjoy Churches* and told of his time spent on committees with JB.
19/03/93	Visit and Talk	St Pancras and The Artworkers' Guild, London	A guided tour of the repairs and remains of St Pancras Chambers and Midland Hotel by Margaret Davies of 'The Conservation Practice'. In the evening she gave a talk on its restoration at The Artworkers' Guild, Queens Gate.
18/05/93	Fourth AGM	Highgate Literary and Scientific Institute, London	Chairman Philippa Davies. An opportunity to view the most precious items in their Betjeman archive. Visit to both eastern and western sections of Highgate Cemetery.
17/06/93	Recital during Chelsea Arts festival	Holy Trinity, Sloane Street, London	*A Church Celebration* devised by Mervyn, Lord Horder and performed by Mervyn and his musicians. Rev. Keith Yates, Tim Heath, Philippa Davies, Kay Jackman and Robert Shaw recited poetry.
24-27/9/93	Society weekend	Oulton Broad, Norfolk	Organised and led by Jonathan Fryer. From Oulton Broad out to Letheringsett, Salle, Winburgh Shelton and Bedingham and Ranworth.

DATE	EVENT	PLACE	PARTICULARS
17/10/93	Fifth Birthday Lecture during literary festival	The Old School Room, Canterbury	Irene Slade with Christopher Nicholson for the Canterbury Festival: *Dangerous Liaisons Overcome*.

1994

DATE	EVENT	PLACE	PARTICULARS
02/02/94	DIY poetry reading	Durning Lawrence Library, Senate House, London University	In combination with the London Society. The first of a series of meetings which have generated recitals of poetry and prose, personal recollections and, occasionally, own compositions of poetry of wide and entertaining variety.
09/03/94	Spring Dinner and film preview	Royal Overseas League, Piccadilly, London	Welcome by Philippa Davies, Grace By Gerry Bishton and Toast by Lord Horder. Peter Gammond presented his film *Betjeman's Britain*.
09/05-03/06/94	Exhibition launch	Senate House, London University	*Oxford Marmalade and a Slim Volume*. The Exhibition ran for over three weeks to mark ten years since Betjeman's death.
09/05/94	Talk	The Chancellor's Hall, Senate Hse, London	Frank Delaney lectured on *Betjeman and Brand Names*. Wine reception followed.
14/05/94	Requiem Mass, lunch, poetry reading and tea	SS Peter and Paul, Wantage	Service led by Father Jonathan Salter commemorating 10 years since JB died, followed by lunch at Old Church House and tea at The Mead, with Cobhams.
19/05/94	A day of celebration. 12 hour reading and dinner	Charing Cross Hotel, London	Tim Heath introduced Nigel Hawthorne who read continuously round the clock to celebrate Betjeman, ten years after his death. Dinner was taken in the Betjeman Carvery. A Society exhibition of Betjeman was set up in the foyer and Tim Heath was the speaker.
09/07/94	Fifth AGM	Globe Theatre Museum, Bear Gardens. Southwark, London	Chairman Philippa Davies. The AGM was held in the Theatre. The Council were on the stage and members in the stalls. Following the AGM there was a visit to see progress in building the new Globe Theatre (three bays of the proposed round theatre were almost complete).
07/08/94	Walk	Pinner, Middx	*Pinner* Led by Ted Griffin.
04/09/94	Car Tour	Middlesex	George Peche, who had been a journalist in the area, guided us around T*he Lost Villages of Heathrow, Harmondsworth, Stanwell, Cranford, Harlington and Colnbrook*.
29/09/94	Society weekend	Gloucestershire and Oxfordshire	Jonathan Fryer organised visits to Badminton, Kelmscott, Ashdown House. Accommodation was at Sudbury House Hotel, Farringdon.
03/10/94	Sixth Birthday Lecture and party	Queen's College, Harley St., London	Sir Kenneth Baker [now Lord Baker] spoke on *Betjeman's Women*. A wine reception followed.
16/10/94	Lecture during the Literary Festival	The Old School Room, Canterbury	John Heath Stubbs spoke on *Betjeman as I Knew Him* for our contribution in the Canterbury Festival.

1995

DATE	EVENT	PLACE	PARTICULARS
08/02/95	DIY poetry reading	Durning Lawrence Library, Senate House, London	The annual traditional combined meeting with the London Society. Members' own choice of readings.

EVENTS: Diary 1987-2008

DATE	EVENT	PLACE	PARTICULARS
29/03/95	Walk and dinner	City of London	From the Barbican to Betjeman's Wine Bar via Charterhouse Square, Clerkenwell Green, Smithfield and 'Barts' Hospital. Walk devised and guided by Gayne Wells.
03/04/95	Visit and joint meeting	London	Joint meeting with the Victorian Society began with a tour of Linley Sambourne House followed by a selection of poetry chosen and read by the members for the members. Refreshments were served in the drawing room.
22/04/95	Church visit	Essex	Gerry Bishton led a tour of Great Warley Church and Brentwood RC Cathedral.
07/06/95	Sixth AGM	Sutton House, Hackney, London	Chairman Philippa Davies. The AGM was followed by a tour of this recently refurbished National Trust property, Sutton House.
21/09/95	Society weekend	Lincolnshire	Jonathan Fryer organised all the accommodation and house and church visits.
25/09/95	Seventh Birthday Lecture and party	King's College, The Strand, London	Anthony Barnes described his father's friendship with Betjeman and his memories of their times together in a style of Desert Island Discs.
07/10/95	Lecture and recital	National Portrait Gallery, London	The Director of the National Portrait Gallery welcomed the Society. Peter Gammond gave a lecture *Highways and Byways* with Anna Gammond and John Heald reading the poems.

1996

DATE	EVENT	PLACE	PARTICULARS
14/01/96	Bookfair and lunch	Haleswood, Canterbury	Buffet lunch was followed by a Bookfair and silent auction of books.
20/02/96	DIY poetry reading	Durning Lawrence Library, Senate House, London	*Favourite Words*. Members' own choice of readings. The annual meeting with the London Society.
10/03/96	Visit	Oxford	Anthony Thorn organised a visit to the Dragon School, North Oxford and to Magdalen College. President of Magdalen, Anthony Smith, introduced Society members to the College and library and a selection of their treasures. Barbara Lynam was guest of honour at tea at the home of Anthony and Gilly Thorn.
15/06/96	Seventh AGM	Union Chapel, Islington, London	Chairman Philippa Davies. The AGM was followed by a walk around Islington led by Gayne Wells.
04/07/96	Visit	Saltwood Castle Hythe	Jane & Alan Clark gave a guided tour of the castle and the library. Members were free to explore the ramparts and gardens. Tea was made and served by Jane.
15/10/96	Performance during Literary Festival	The Gulbenkian Theatre Canterbury	*Betjemania* devised and led by David Benedictus with David Gould on the piano for the Canterbury Festival. A party at Haleswood followed.
11/11/96	Service of Memorialisaton and Reception	Westminster Abbey, London	A ceremony to celebrate Sir John Betjeman's memorialisation in Poet's Corner, Westminster Abbey, in recognition of his contribution to English Literature, led by the Dean, The Very Reverend Michael Mayne. Patrick Leigh Fermor gave the address and Joanna Lumley read from JB's

EVENTS: Diary 1987-2008

DATE	EVENT	PLACE	PARTICULARS
			Collected Poems. Lady Wilson unveiled the cartouche which had been designed by Donald Buttress with lettering by David Peace. Candida Lycett Green's grandchildren laid flowers. A reception at the Vitello D'Oro, Great Smith Street, completed the celebration.
12/11/96	Eighth Birthday Lecture and party	King's College, London	Lady Wilson spoke, celebrating Betjeman's 90th birthday; she recalled her friendship with JB and their mutual love of words and rhyme.
16/11/96	Visit	Whitechapel Bell Foundry, London	Mr Hughes, Director of the Whitechapel Bell Foundry led a tour of the Foundry and showed examples of new bells being cast and old favourites being repaired.
20/11/96	Inauguration of the Oxford Branch	North Oxford	Anthony Thorn invited friends and contacts in Oxford, and Society and Council members to his home in Oxford to form the Oxford Branch.
1997			
11/02/97	Talk	Durning Lawrence Library, Senate House, London	Mervyn, Lord Horder spoke on *The Curiosities of Publishing* recalling his time at Duckworth's Publishing House.
20/03/97	Visit	Uffington	Lunch at Garrards Farm. A short walk to the Tom Brown's Schooldays Museum and tea at Candida Lycett Green's house with reminiscences from Ron Liddiard, Mary Matthews, Betty Marchant, Marcella Shaw and Jim Smith. Candida read from her own hand-written copy of *Archie and the Strict Baptists*.
01/04/97	Publication		*A Bibliographical Companion to Betjeman* by Peter Gammond, with assistance from John Heald, was published to critical acclaim.
10/04/97	DIY poetry reading	Durning Lawrence Library, Senate House, London	Annual joint meeting with the London Society. Members' choice of *Favourite Words*.
21/06/97	Eighth AGM	Central Hall, Westminster, London	Peter Gammond was elected Chairman in succession to Philippa Davies. Members enjoyed a tour of the Abbey including the Jerusalem Chamber and Poets' Corner.
23/09/97	Ninth Birthday Lecture and party	King's College, London	David Peace was the Birthday guest. He described his friendship with Betjeman and the making of the chapter on Staffordshire in Collins Guide to English Parish Churches. JB admired David's wife, Jean, for her art and writing.
18/10/97	Walk	Chelsea, London	Andrew Davies led the group around *Literary Nooks and Crannies of Chelsea*.
08/11/97	Inauguration of the Shires Branch	Vaughan College, Leicester	The Shires Branch was formed. Baz Morris was elected Chairman.
1998			
24/02/98	Lecture	Durning Lawrence Library, Senate House, London	John Heald presented *Mervyn Horder: A Celebration* in honour of our late lamented President.
12/03/98	DIY poetry reading	Durning Lawrence Library, Senate House, London	Combined meeting with the London Society. Members' own choice of readings *Worth Repeating*.

A scrapbook of the first twenty years

EVENTS: *Diary 1987-2008*

DATE	EVENT	PLACE	PARTICULARS
26/03/98	Talk and film show	The Run Run Shaw Theatre, Piccadilly, London	Eddie Mirzoeff and the production team of *A Passion for Churches* for the BBC described the creation of this film and screened it in its entirety.
06/06/98	Ninth AGM	The House Mill, Bow, London	Chairman Peter Gammond. A tour of The House Mill was followed by tea.
30/06/98	Visit	Marlborough College, Wiltshire	The Archivist, Terry Rogers, guided us around The College, the Boarding Houses, the playing fields and chapel. A detour to Mildenhall church was arranged on the homeward journey.
23/09/98	10th Birthday Lecture and party	King's College, London	Bevis Hillier was the Birthday speaker.
21/11/98	10th Anniversary of the Society Champagne reception and grand celebration dinner	Butcher's Hall, St Bartholomew Close, London	A dinner to celebrate Ten Years of the Betjeman Society in the presence of our President, Lady Wilson. Gerry Bishton said grace. Chairman Peter Gammond welcomed the guests, Founder, Philippa Davies replied. Candida Lycett Green also spoke.

1999

DATE	EVENT	PLACE	PARTICULARS
10/02/99	DIY poetry reading	Durning Lawrence Library, Senate House, London	Members' own choice of readings with the London Society. *A Way With Words*.
14/04/99	10th Anniversary walk and dinner	Lincoln's Inn Fields, London	Continuing the year of celebration Gayne Wells led a walk round the Inns of Court followed by dinner.
15/05/99	Visit	Southend	*A wide Prospect of Sea and Sky* Diane Simpson led a tour of Southend viewing the promenade, the town, Royal Parade, houses of literary characters and a ride on the train, The Sir John Betjeman, along Southend pier.
15/06/99	Visit	Isle of Man	Erin Arts Centre was the venue of the formation of the new Isle of Man Branch in the presence of Prunella Scales and Timothy West.
20/06/99	Inauguration of the Isle of Man Branch	The British Library, St Pancras, London	A tour of the new British Library at St Pancras and a display of some of their Betjeman archive.
26/06/99	10th AGM	Vaughan College, Leicester	Chairman Peter Gammond. The Shires Branch hosted the day. Welcome by Baz Morris, lectures by Ken Webb and John Florance, with contributions from other members of the Shires Branch. There was an opportunity to join walking tours of the city.
30/07/99	Court & Social	Buckingham Palace	The Chairman headed a party of Council members and vice-president Bevis Hillier when the Society was invited to a Royal Garden Party.
30/09/99	11th Birthday Lecture and party	King's College, London	Auberon Waugh was the Birthday guest. He pleaded for the cause of rhyming poetry.
17/11/99	Presentation	Durning Lawrence Library, Senate House, London	John Heald presented *Private Views,* his choice of poetry, letters and prose with Peter and Anna Gammond.

2000

DATE	EVENT	PLACE	PARTICULARS
20/01/00	Visit	London	Visit to the Lord Chancellor's residence at the Palace of Westminster.
09/02/00	DIY poetry reading	Senate House, London	Joint annual meeting with the London Society. Members' readings of *Right Lines*.

DATE	EVENT	PLACE	PARTICULARS
28/03/00	Presentation	Ealing Town Hall	Joint meeting with the Ealing Museum, Art and History Society. Introduction of the Betjeman Society by Peter Gammond.
04/04/00	Visit	London	Second visit to the Lord Chancellor's Residence at the Palace of Westminster.
08/04/00	Coach tour	London	*Betjeman's London* led by Gayne Wells.
23/04/00	Joint meeting and performance	Grantchester, Cambridge	A day with the Rupert Brooke Society. Mark Peyton performed. *The Old Vicarage Grantchester.* Presentations of poetry by Tim Heath, Peter and Anna Gammond, and John Heald.
03/05/00	Visit	London	Guided tour of the St Pancras Chambers.
17/05/00	Visit	London	By popular demand a second guided tour of the St Pancras Chambers.
10/06/00	11th AGM	Digby Hall, Sherborne	Chairman Peter Gammond. A day with the Sherborne Branch organised by Kay Jackman. The AGM in the flower-filled hall was followed by an exhibition and lunch. Jonathan Stedall shared reminiscences and screened his BBC film of his tour with JB. Tea was followed by a guided tour around the Abbey.
15/09/00	Visit	Oxfordshire	Guided tour of William Morris's house, Kelmscott Manor.
28/09/00	12th Birthday Lecture and party	St John's church, Waterloo, London	Andrew Motion, the Poet Laureate was the guest speaker reading some of his own verse and recalling his links with Larkin.
19/11/00	First Vice Presidents' cocktail party, lunch and book fair	Haleswood, Canterbury	Sherry was served from a 'Betjeman Patent' tantalus. Books were displayed in preparation for the afternoon auction. Cream tea was served before departure.

2001

DATE	EVENT	PLACE	PARTICULARS
13/01/01	Performance of poetry	Charlton House, London	Joint meeting with the Woolwich and District Antiquarian Society.
07/03/01	DIY poetry reading	Senate House, London	Joint meeting with the London Society. *Ways with Words.* Members' own choice of readings.
26/04/01	Visit	Spitalfields, London	Talk and tour of the premises of Society for Protection of Ancient Buildings.
01/05/01	Visit	Oxfordshire	Sezincote, house and garden.
10/06/01	12th AGM	Ardington House, Oxfordshire	Chairman Peter Gammond. The meeting took place at the home of the Baring family. The Wantage Branch hosted the day.
23/08/01	13th Birthday Lecture and party	St John's Waterloo, London	Patrick Garland was the guest speaker.
29/09/01	Visit	Kinlet Hall Shropshire	David Engleheart, pupil of JB, invited the Society to Moffats School. His family and staff hosted the day. Joint recital of readings. Visit to the church.
20/10/01	Visit and talk	Notting Hill, London	Elizabeth, Lady Longford invited the Society to her home. She spoke and answered questions.
15/11/01	Entertainment	Senate House, London	*Betjeman's Humour.* A presentation devised and delivered by John Heald.

EVENTS: *Diary 1987-2008*

DATE	EVENT	PLACE	PARTICULARS
14/12/01	Royal visit	Dorchester	The Prince of Wales accepted an invitation by the Sherborne Branch to attend their recital of poetry *Moments of Vision* in aid of Breakthrough Breast Cancer at St. Mary's Church, Dorchester.

2002

DATE	EVENT	PLACE	PARTICULARS
28/01/02	Talk and exhibition	The Poetry Library, Royal Festival Hall, London	Mary Enright, Librarian, was host and speaker.
19/02/02	DIY poetry reading	Durning Lawrence Library, Senate House, London	Annual joint meeting with the London Society *A Word in Your Ear*. Members' choice of readings.
21/03/02	Talk	St John's, Waterloo, London	*Betjeman Illustrated in a Series of Views* by R.M. Healey, author of a Shell Guide to Hertfordshire.
11/05/02	Coach tour	London and Metroland	A Visit to Metroland following the route of JB's film and visiting various locations led by Gayne Wells.
08/06/02	13th AGM	Highgate, London	John Heald elected Chairman in succession to Peter Gammond. Gwynydd Gosling organised an exhibition and Dorothy Sweet spoke. A walking tour of Highgate followed.
13/07/02	Visit and tour	Canterbury	John and Maureen Ingram, Canterbury Cathedral and City guides, led members on a tour. Organised by the Canterbury Branch.
28/08/02	14th Birthday Lecture and party	St. John's, Waterloo, London	Dr. Jim Gibson was the guest speaker.
07/09/02	Visit	Harwich	*From Flea Pit to Picture Palace*. Films and lecture by Andrew Davies at the Electric Theatre Cinema and tour of the town.
06/11/02	Talk and unveiling	St John's, Waterloo, London	*Betjeman in Sight and Sound*. A programme of the poet on TV, wireless and recordings, devised and delivered by Peter Gammond. Unveiling of Grahame Laver's portrait of Sir John Betjeman by Lady Wilson.

2003

DATE	EVENT	PLACE	PARTICULARS
04/02/03	DIY poetry reading	Durning Lawrence Library, Senate House, London	Joint annual meeting with the London Society. *Words of Honour*. Members' own choice of readings.
18/03/03	Talk	Senate House, London	*Sir John's Railway Stations*. An illustrated talk by Andrew Davies.
12/04/03	Coach tour	Oxfordshire & Berkshire	*Oxfordshire Revisited*. A tour of Betjeman country organised by Mike Wilson.
27/04/03	Readings	Arundel, Sussex	*An Evening with Betjeman* at Boxgrove Priory. One of a series of presentations by invitation, devised and performed by Peter and Anna Gammond and John Heald in aid of a chosen charity.
21/05/03	Walking tour	City of London	*Toddling Along From the Barbican*. A London walk led by Gayne Wells.
07/06/03	14th AGM	The Lawn, Lincoln	Chairman John Heald. Entertainment by the Shires Branch followed by a tour of Lincoln City and Cathedral. Hosted by the Lincolnshire Branch.

EVENTS: *Diary 1987-2008*

DATE	EVENT	PLACE	PARTICULARS
12/07/03	Bookfair and Auction	Sherborne	Kay Jackman and members of the Sherborne Branch hosted the day in the Digby Hall. Auctioneer John Heald
28/08/03	15th Birthday Lecture and party	St John's, Waterloo, London	Jonathan Stedall was the guest speaker.
25/09/03	Talk	Senate House, London	*Two Columns of an Arch.* A celebration of John and Myfanwy Piper by Geoffrey Elborn and R.M.Healey.
24/11/03	Talk	St John's Waterloo, London	*Betjeman in Sight and Sound, Part 2.* A programme of the poet on T.V., wireless and film, devised and delivered by Peter Gammond.

2004

DATE	EVENT	PLACE	PARTICULARS
09/03/04	DIY poetry reading	Senate House, London	Joint annual meeting with the London Society. *Wise Words* Members' own choice of readings.
21/04/04	Lecture	The Gallery, Cowcross St., London	*Stylistic Cold Wars - Betjeman versus Pevsner* by Dr Timothy Mowl, Architectural Historian.
19-20/05/04	Visit	North Cornwall	To commemorate the 20th Anniversary of Sir John's death. Places visited included Trebetherick, Padstow, St Ervan and Wadebridge.
19/06/04	15th AGM	Art Workers' Guild, Queen's Sq., London	Chairman John Heald. AGM followed by a talk.
17/07/04	Visit	West Dean, Sussex	Tour of the house and garden of the former home of Edward James.
23/08/04	16th Birthday Lecture and party	St John's, Waterloo, London	Talk by John Julius Norwich. *Memories of travels with Betjeman.*
25/09//04	Visit	Diss	Train from Liverpool Street to Diss and visit of the town in the company of President Mary, Lady Wilson
11/12/04	Visit and Talk	Holy Trinity Church, Sloane Street, London	Talk by Dr Mary Cotterell of the Arts and Crafts Guild and tour of the church followed by tea at the Cadogan Hotel.

2005

DATE	EVENT	PLACE	PARTICULARS
08/02/05	DIY poetry reading	Senate House, London	Joint annual meeting with the London Society. *Word of Mouth.* Members own choice of readings.
05/04/05	Talk	St Mary Aldermary, London	*Betjeman's London.* An illustrated talk by Andrew Davies. Joint event with The Friends of City Churches to celebrate 40th Anniversary of Betjeman's Pitkin Guide.
14/05/05	Visit	Swindon	Tour of the town and its history and churches with Father Jonathan Salter, Roy Denison and the Wantage Branch.
18/06/05	16th AGM	Canterbury	Chairman John Heald. Tour of the Deanery with the Dean, The Very Reverend Robert Willis, tour of St Alphege and St Martin's churches and the King's School with Ken Pinnock. Talk by Prof Mike Irwin at the Dominican Priory. Hosted by the Canterbury Branch
16/07/05	Tour	Brighton	*Betjeman's Brighton.* Visits to churches and meeting Revd. Gerard Irvine.
22/08/05	17th Birthday Lecture and party	St John's, Waterloo, London	Talk by Janie Hampton, friend of Betjeman, about her biography and recollections of Joyce Grenfell.

A scrapbook of the first twenty years

EVENTS: *Diary 1987-2008*

DATE	EVENT	PLACE	PARTICULARS
13-18/09/05	Visit	Isle of Man	AGM of the Isle of Man Branch. Chairman, John Bethell, Sec/Treas Joyce Corlett, Invitation to tea with The Governor and Mrs Macfadyen. Steam train journey and tour of the island.
24/09/05	Visit	Hull	Joint meeting with The Philip Larkin Society. Tour of the town and important Larkin landmarks in Hull guided by Paul Walker and Amber Allcroft. Visit to the university library welcomed by Betty Mackereth and Judy Burg.
26/11/05	Presentation of archive	Highgate, London	Official presentation of Grahame Laver's portrait of JB and handover of Society collection to the Highgate Literary and Scientific Institute.
2006			
07/02/06	DIY poetry readings	Senate House, London	Joint meeting with London Society. Members' choice of readings.
09/04/06	Tour by coach	Oxford	*Betjeman's Oxford*, including Keble, St Barnabas and Magdalen.
06/05/06	Book launch	Lincolnshire	Reception and lunch at Sausthorpe Old Hall to celebrate the publication of *Betjeman's Lincolnshire*.
16/06/06	Visit	Highgrove	Council members invited in the centenary year.
17/06/06	17th AGM	Kensington & Chelsea Town Hall, London	Chairman John Heald. Visit to Leighton House hosted by the curator, Daniel Robbins.
22/06/06	Talk	Art Workers' Guild, London	Hermione Hobhouse, one-time Secretary of the Victorian Society, shared her memories.
24/06/06	Unveiling of Blue Plaque	Garrards' Farm, Uffington	Performed by Pam Ayres at the Betjemans' former home. She read her poem *On White Horse Hill*.
27/07/06	Talk	The Gallery, Cowcross St., London	*Betjeman and the BBC*. Stephen Games, author of '*Trains and Buttered Toast*', talked about his compilation of the book.
28/08/06	Service of dedication	Westminster Abbey, London	A celebration of the centenary of the birth of JB. Bevis Hillier gave the address, Lady Wilson laid a posy in Poets' Corner. Chairman John Heald read.
09/09/06	Dinner and 18th Birthday Party	Butchers' Hall, City of London	Celebration dinner. Colin Wright said grace, John Heald was MC. Lady Wilson, Eddie Mirzoeff, Ken Pinnock, Peter Gammond and Philippa Davies spoke.
15/09/06	Unveiling of Blue Plaque	31 Highgate West Hill, London	David Canadine and Andrew Motion spoke and John Murray unveiled English Heritage's contribution to recognise JB's former home. Tea at Highgate Literary and Scientific Institute.
28-29/10/06	Weekend	York	Talk by Richard Hardy & film show at York Railway Museum. Dinner at Bedern Hall, City tour with Daniel Buttery.
25/11/06	Unveiling of Society plaque	St Anne's Highgate, London	The plaque in the church where JB was baptised was unveiled by Philippa Davies and blessed by Canon John Beckwith.
2007			
06/03/07	Readings	Senate House, London	Joint meeting with the London Society. *Words Galore*. Members' choice of poetry and prose.
19/05/07	Literary outing	Oxford	A day with the Larkin Society in Oxford guided by Bernard Richards.

90 *A scrapbook of the first twenty years*

DATE	EVENT	PLACE	PARTICULARS
18/06/07	18th AGM	Angel Hotel, Market Harborough	Chairman John Heald. Hosted by The Shires Branch. Bevis Hillier ratified as President. Visits to Congregational Church and Foxton Locks or film show.
21/07/07	Tour on foot and by train	London termini	*London's historic railway stations North of the Thames*, led by Don Kennedy.
04/09/07	19th Birthday Lecture and party	St John's, Waterloo, London	Imogen Lycett Green was the birthday guest, in conversation with John Heald.
25/10/07	Lecture	The Gallery, Cowcross St., London	Dr John Florance illustrated *The Voices of Betjeman* with readings, film clips and sound recordings.
12/11/07	Unveiling of sculpture	St Pancras station, London	The sculpture of JB by Martin Jennings was unveiled by Andrew Motion and Candida Lycett Green, celebrating the opening of the refurbished station.

2008

DATE	EVENT	PLACE	PARTICULARS
11/03/08	DIY poetry readings	Senate House, London	*I know what I like.* Members' own choice of readings.
17/04/08	Films	Senate House, London	*A Time for Dance.* Films of poems performed by The Australian Ballet. JB's words to Jim Parker's music.
17/05/08	Book fair, lunch and visit	Canterbury	Hosted by the Davies family. Auctioneer of books John Heald. Visit to St Augustine's Abbey led by Martin Taylor. Tea with talk by Kenneth Pinnock followed by visit to original Cathedral water cisterns.
14/06/08	Tour on foot and by train	London termini	*London's Historic Railway Stations south of the Thames* organised by Don Kennedy.
21/06/08	19th AGM	Union Jack Club, London	David Pattison elected Chairman in succession to John Heald. The AGM was followed by a preview of the show *The Best of Betjeman* by Lance Pierson prior to performance at the Edinburgh Festival.
28/08/08	Poetry reading	St Pancras station, London	Members gathered round the Martin Jennings statue of JB to read poems.
28/08/08	20th Birthday Lecture and party	St John's, Waterloo, London	An evening of fun and *The Bonus of Laughter* with Keith Hutton, Richard Morley and Jean Garbutt.
20-21/09/08	Weekend	Norfolk	A tour of the county led by Mike Wilson.
23/10/08	Lecture	The Gallery, Cowcross St., London	Prof Jon Stallworthy spoke on *Betjeman's Ancestral Voices.*
21/11/08	20th Anniversary Celebration	Old Synagogue, Canterbury	*Afternoon Teacakes and Scones* hosted by the Canterbury Branch. A grand party, twenty years to the day since the founding of the Society.

GALLERY

Lady Wilson, Canon Robert Wright and Chairman John Heald at the service of rededication at Westminster Abbey, 2006

Photograph courtesy of Bernard Mattimore

Dick Squires leaning on a Sarsen Stone in Betjeman Park, Wantage

Twentieth Aniversary Party.
Afternoon Teacakes and Scones at the Old Synagogue, Canterbury. November 21st 2008. Bevis Hillier holding a minature sculpture of JB at St. Pancras and Sarah Taylor reciting her poem.
Professor Mike Irwin addressing the 16th AGM in Canterbury.

Photograph courtesy of Bernard Mattimore

92 A scrapbook of the first twenty years

EPILOGUE

Bevis Hillier

I was a friend of John Betjeman in the thirteen years – lucky thirteen – between 1971 and his death in 1984. Apart from his family, I must be one of the few people now living who knew him well – though my contemporary and friend Dominick Harrod (whose mother was briefly engaged to JB) knew him far longer, as did Mark Girouard, Barry Humphries, Eddie Mirzoeff, John Nankivell, Dick Squires and Jonathan Stedall; and at least one person survives who is mentioned in *Summoned by Bells* (1960) – the Revd. Prebendary Gerard Irvine, who first met JB in the 1930's.

It was a great privilege to know JB. Meeting some writers adds nothing to what one gains from their writings – indeed, they can be a positive disappointment. It was not so with JB. You experienced the spontaneity of his wit. As you passed buildings with him, he directed you what to look at – things you would never have noticed yourself. Above all, it was always a two-way traffic: he responded to *you*, wanted to know all about you. (He was one of two great writers I have met – Iris Murdoch was the other – in whom you not only wanted to confide, you felt it was a duty. One experience of mine that I retailed to JB, he put in one of his poems – I'd rather not say which, but will reveal it in my autobiography, *Betraying Myself*, still in its early stages.)

Being President of the Betjeman Society is another privilege. It gives me the chance to pay tribute to the extraordinary woman who founded it, Philippa Davies. Many people in the Society have said the same thing: 'If JB had ever met her, he would have fallen desperately in love with her.' She is the strong tennis girl of his dreams: an English beauty who combines vivacity with efficiency. It would in no way hurt that she is a physiotherapist. In his later years, JB had a physiotherapist. She was a rather severe lady, not in her first youth; but he christened her establishment 'Madame Venus's Massage Parlour'. Philippa would have been much more his cup of tea. And Jake has been her invaluable Denis Thatcher.

The story of the naughty stratagem by which she came to found the Society twenty years ago is a minor comic masterpiece – and she tells it, with appealing self-deprecation, in the early part of this Scrapbook. I once tried an artful dodge of that sort. For five years I lived in Los Angeles, working on the *Los Angeles Times*. I had a great yearning to meet Fred Astaire, whose films with Ginger Rogers I think the summit of animated Art Deco. So I wrote him a letter beginning: 'The late Duke of Windsor told me, "If ever you are in Los Angeles, you should look up my old friend Fred Astaire …"' I had not known the Duke, though he was a member of my London club. Astaire telephoned me, when I was sunbathing on the verandah outside my house. He was polite and charming, but I realized I was rumbled when I was unable to give a convincing answer to the question, 'And how is the Duchess, now?'" The meeting did not take place. I failed: but Philippa's daring ruse succeeded – and how!

It has become a wonderful, friendly Society, with fascinating meetings and one of the best magazines issued by a literary society. The other people – besides Philippa – who deserve to be thanked have been acknowledged in this book; and my task, in this Epilogue, is less to dwell on the past than to look to the future.

Our membership numbers are healthy; but at more than one meeting I have urged members (and I learn from this book that I am not the first to do so) to try to recruit one new member from among their friends. It is not just that one wants more people to share in the varied pleasures that the Betjeman Society offers. Wise people look ahead to rainy days. More members mean more subscriptions. The day may come when the Society collectively decides it needs to fight a campaign: and in fighting campaigns, money is power. I mean, supposing that by some odious tidying-up scheme it were decided that the magnificent statue of JB should be removed from St Pancras Station. (Impossible? – don't forget what happened to the Euston Arch.) Wouldn't we want to protest? Wouldn't we want to campaign? New *young* members are what we need most.

At the same two meetings, I hope with not too distasteful a touch of the macabre, I asked that members might remember the Society in their wills. I ask it again, now. In my more ambitious pipe-dreams, I even envisage, one day, a London club-room for members, with a refrigerator stocked with decent wines – though one of the Society's officers tartly commented that that was probably 'a fridge too far'.

New members or no new members; munificent bequests or no bequests, I know that we shall continue to do what Philippa and her co-conspirators set out to do all those years ago – as John Heald (to whom, also, we owe so much) summarizes it, 'to promote the study and appreciation of Betjeman's life and work ... [and also to be] a fan club'. If we were to use exalted language and to be a little pompous, we might claim to be keepers of the Betjeman flame. That *is* an aim. But if we were to be more down-to-earth and honest, we might say: 'We intend to go on enjoying ourselves to the utmost, with the continued help of one of the greatest literary life-enhancers who ever lived.'

Synopsis of life of Sir John Betjeman

Bill Pickard

1906 John Betjeman was born on 28th August at Brookfield Mansions, Highgate, London. His father was a cabinet maker and he was expected to go into 'trade'.
1908 His family moved to 31 West Hill, Highgate, a modest villa in a prosperous road.

1910-11 Mrs Bouman, their next-door neighbour, encouraged him with poetry and verse. He suffered domestic punishments at the hands of the Betjeman's Calvinistic housemaid, named Maud.
1912-15 JB attended Byron House, a 'Montessori Method' school (run by two sisters) where he flourished in the arts and produced verses for his teacher. *"When I grow up. I am going to have long hair and be a poet"* (JB aged 8).
1915 He moved on to Highgate Junior School. Discipline was sadistic and the educational standard not high. He showed his poems to T.S.Eliot who was one of his teachers.
1917 JB was sent as a boarder to the Dragon School, Oxford (run by the Lynam family). It was a liberal and radical school. John did much poetry, acting and mimicry. He stayed there until the summer of 1920 (aged 14) and it was one of the great formative influences of his life.

1920 The Betjeman family moved to 53 Church Street, Chelsea: 'a Georgian box'. JB was by now particularly interested in architecture, especially churches. In September 1920 he became a boarder at Marlborough College, Wiltshire where Arthur Elton, Louis MacNeice, and Anthony Blunt were fellow pupils.
1921 JB had his first verses published, winning prizes for them. He was a talented actor and became a regular contributor to *The Marlburian* and *The Heretick* (an 'Arties versus Hearties' magazine founded by a rich scholar). JB's acting attracted brilliant reviews but his education was haphazard. He only just scraped into Oxford as a fee-paying student.
1925-29 Life began for JB as an undergraduate at Magdalen College, Oxford, where Joseph Addison and Oscar Wilde had both studied. He met many rich, titled and famous people and gained a 'unique' place among them; much admired for his originality of mind. Lifelong friendships were made. JB detested his English tutor, C.S. Lewis, who may have been one of the reasons why he adopted High Anglicanism. He edited the magazine *'Cherwell'* but left Oxford without a degree. From 1926 onward, JB often stayed with Oxford friends, many of whom were members of the landed aristocracy, owning stately homes in England, Wales, Scotland and Ireland.

APPENDIX: Synopsis of JB's life

1930-31 JB had a brief career as a prep. schoolmaster, followed by a job on the *Architectural Review*. Edward James published *Mount Zion*. This was his first book of poems. He was, by then, a prolific writer of verse and prose.

1932 When JB was assistant editor of the *Architectural Review* he was shown an article on Indian temples by a girl called Penelope Chetwode (her father was a Field Marshal in command of the Army Forces in India).

1933 They fell in love, and had an amazing on-off courtship which resulted in a clandestine marriage and difficulties until the two families accepted it. The newly-weds each expected a large measure of independence in marriage. Chapman and Hall published *Ghastly Good Taste*.

1934 J and PB moved to Uffington, Berkshire, where he was churchwarden. They had stables and horses, and they drank milk from their own goat. Many of the rich and famous came to visit them at Uffington.

1937 Publication of *Continual Dew*. This began JB's link with John Murray (the publisher).

1938 Their first child, Paul, was born at Uffington (Paul now lives in New York). JB made his first television appearance (at the old Alexandra Palace).

1939 Having failed an RAF medical examination, JB was found war-work in films for the Ministry of Information. Laurie Lee and John Mortimer were also there at that time.

1940 *Old Lights for New Chancels* was published.

1941 JB was posted to Dublin as Press attaché to the British Representative. He and his family lived in a faded Georgian mansion in Collinstown, near Dublin. JB learnt Irish, 'met the people' and had the friendship of President de Valera. He met Joan Hunter Dunn at the Ministry of Information in London.

1942 A daughter, Candida, was born in Dublin. She became a renowned beauty and edited her father's letters.

1943 JB became a regular on the radio and one of the question masters on the 'Brains Trust'. J and PB were invited to the marriage of Joan Hunter Dunn but were unable to accept the invitation.

1945 *New Bats in Old Belfries* was published. JB and family moved to the seventeenth-century 'Old Rectory', Farnborough, Berkshire (a 'William and Mary' house on the Downs above Wantage). The Betjeman's factory in London and the family business were closed and sold.

1946-47 JB had a minor operation at the Acland Hospital, Oxford, where his nurse was Mary Renault, the writer of ancient classical fact/fiction. He became a champion of 'all things Victorian' and was lampooned for it.

1948 PB became a Roman Catholic and went back to India to find temples. *Selected Poems* was published.

1949 Osbert Lancaster and other more serious artists began to draw and paint JB.

1950 JB did editorial work for *Time and Tide* as 'literary advisor'.

1951 The Betjeman family moved to 'The Mead', Wantage (on the site of King Alfred's palace).

APPENDIX: Synopsis of JB's life

1952-53 JB was beginning to be well known on television. He was sacked as literary editor of *Time and Tide* and wrote *Caprice* on Lady Rhondda.

1954 JB bought a City of London house at 43 Cloth Fair (now 'Betjeman's Wine Bar'). *A Few Late Chrysanthemums*, *Poems in the Porch* and *Diary of a Church Mouse* were all published this year.

1955-57 JB spent a lot of time in London broadcasting and PB spent much time away in far-off places.

1957 JB was appointed Visiting Professor at the University of Cincinnati, U.S.A.

1958 *John Betjeman's Collected Poems* (John Murray) became a runaway best-seller.

1959 PB by now was spending most of her time in India studying temples, etc.

1960 JB went to Australia (much Victoriana) and made a television series about it. He was also an official guest at the marriage of Princess Margaret and Anthony Armstrong-Jones.

1967 JB attended a Memorial Service for John Masefield, (Poet Laureate) but Cecil Day-Lewis was chosen to succeed Masefield. Day-Lewis had only a few years left to live.

1969 Sir John Betjeman was knighted by Queen Elizabeth II (at 63 years of age).

1970s JB made many remarkable films for television such as *Metroland*.

1972 The Betjeman's left the Mead, Wantage. PB moved to Wales. Cecil Day-Lewis died and JB was appointed Poet Laureate on 10th October 1972.

1973 JB moved to Radnor Walk, London.

1979 JB made his last visit to Ireland, to Letterkenny, Co. Donegal and had his portrait painted by Derek Hill.

1980 *"Betjemania"* a revue based on his poems was transferred to New York by Liza Minnelli.

1981 JB developed Parkinson's disease. He wrote very little and lived quietly in Cornwall and London.

1983 JB's last public appearance was in a wheelchair to name a British Rail locomotive 'Sir John Betjeman'. He returned to Trebetherick, Cornwall, the scene of his childhood holidays, where he and Archibald Ormsby-Gore, his famous Teddy bear, received few visitors. Despite care, his health failed.

1984 On 19th May Sir John Betjeman died and on Tuesday 22nd May he was buried on a day of torrential rain in the churchyard of his beloved St. Enodoc church. The coffin-bearers squelched across the golf course, the only access to the church.

GALLERY

*Clockwise from top:
Michael Richardson at work editing the Scrapbook 2008;
Clive Murphy enjoying the Birthday Party, King's College, London 1995;
Gayne Wells wearing JB's boater at the Highgate Literary & Scientific Institute exhibition, 2002;
Society merchandise and Bibliography all in the Society blue with JB logo;
Betjeman Ale beer mat;
The Blue Plaque at Garrards Farm, Uffington which was unveiled by Pam Ayres, 2006*

98 *A scrapbook of the first twenty years*

A brief Betjeman Bibliography

Horace Liberty

A bibliography for inclusion in a book such as *The Betjeman Society Scrapbook* must be, by necessity, brief and incomplete. It is intended to point the general reader in the direction of the main books which contain John Betjeman's verse, prose, and letters, together with a number of biographical and critical studies. For a more complete list, see *A Bibliographical Companion to Betjeman* (The Betjeman Society 1997) and *A Betjeman Checklist* (The Betjeman Society 2006), both compiled by Peter Gammond and John Heald, or *John Betjeman: A Bibliography* by William S Peterson (Oxford University Press 2006).

John Betjeman's Verse
Mount Zion (The James Press 1931) Facsimile reprint 1975
Continual Dew (John Murray 1937) Facsimile reprint 1977
Old Lights for New Chancels (John Murray 1940)
New Bats in Old Belfries (John Murray 1945)
Selected Poems (John Murray 1948)
A Few Late Chrysanthemums (John Murray 1954)
Poems in the Porch (SPCK 1954)
Collected Poems (John Murray 1958) – many reprints and updated editions since first publication. The centenary edition in 2006 included *Summoned by Bells*.
Summoned by Bells (John Murray 1960)
High and Low (John Murray 1966)
A Nip in the Air (John Murray 1974)
The Best of Betjeman (John Murray in association with Penguin Books 1975)
Church Poems (John Murray 1981)
Uncollected Poems (John Murray 1982)

John Betjeman's Prose, Letters and Radio Talks
Ghastly Good Taste (Chapman and Hall 1933) Revised and updated edition 1970 (Anthony Blond)
Cornwall – A Shell Guide (Architectural Press 1934) Revised and updated in 1964 (Faber)
Devon – A Shell Guide (Architectural Press 1936)
An Oxford University Chest (John Miles 1938) Reprinted 1979 (Oxford University Press)
Antiquarian Prejudice (Hogarth Press 1939)
Vintage London (Collins 1942)
English Cities and Small Towns (Collins 1943)
John Piper (Penguin Modern Painters 1944)
First and Last Loves (John Murray 1952)
Collins Guide to English Parish Churches (Collins 1958)

London's Historic Railway Stations (John Murray 1972)
A Pictorial History of English Architecture (John Murray 1972)
Archie and the Strict Baptists (John Murray 1977)
Letters Volume 1: 1926 – 1951, edited by Candida Lycett Green (Methuen 1994)
Letters Volume 2: 1951 - 1984, edited by Candida Lycett Green (Methuen 1995)
Coming Home, an anthology of prose, edited by Candida Lycett Green (Methuen 1997)
Trains and Buttered Toast, edited by Stephen Games (John Murray 2006)
John Betjeman on Trains, edited by Jonathan Glancey (Methuen 2006)
Tennis Whites and Teacakes, edited by Stephen Games (John Murray 2007)
Sweet Songs of Zion, edited by Stephen Games (Hodder and Stoughton 2007)
John Betjeman on Churches, edited by Jonathan Glancey (Methuen 2007)

Biography
John Betjeman - A Study, Derek Stanford (Neville Spearman 1961)
John Betjeman – His Life and Work, Patrick Taylor-Martin (Allen Lane 1983)
John Betjeman – A Life in Pictures, Bevis Hillier (John Murray 1984)
Young Betjeman, Bevis Hillier (John Murray 1988)
John Betjeman, Dennis Brown, in the series Writers and their Work (Northcote House 1999)
John Betjeman – New Fame, New Love, Bevis Hillier (John Murray 2002)
Betjeman – The Bonus of Laughter, Bevis Hillier (John Murray 2004)
Betjeman – The Biography, Bevis Hillier (John Murray 2006)
Betjeman, A N Wilson (Hutchinson 2006)
The Little Book of Betjeman, Peter Gammond (Guidon 2006)

List of Suscribers

Laurence Akehurst
Mr D.W. Armitt
Terence Atkins
Mrs June Attwood
Alan G.E.Bailey
Peter Bainbridge
Roger Beacham
Betty Beale
Peter & Ann Beechey
A.G.Bell
Susan Bitterling
Joan & Peter Blacklock
Mr & Mrs A.G.E.Bond
Mrs Ruth Bond (Widow Packman)
Paul Hollins Booker
Colonel John Brake
William Breare-Hall
Brian & Wendy Brooks
Doreen Browne
Mr M.B.Bunting
Roy Burton
Rodney Callow, Lincoln
Donald Macgregor Campbell
Mrs Yvonne Carey
His Honour Judge Derek Clarkson Q.C.
Ralph Cobham & Susan Cobham
Shirley Cook
Robert Coon
Joyce E. Corlett MBE
Sue Cover
Jake Davies
Philippa Davies
Roy Dean
Richard Patrick Dennis
Roy & Mya Denison
Miss Shirley C.Dex
John Diffey
Reg & Eileen Eden
John Edney
Dr.John A.Florance
Fenella Fraser Ker
Brian Frear
Jonathan Fryer
Peter Gammond
Rick Gekoski
Charles Vincent Gentle
Helen Gibson & James Gibson
Jane Gray
Brian Hacker
John Hallier
David Hamilton
Peter Hann
Mrs Nancy Harris
John & Maggie Harris
Michael Hartwell
John & Ann Heald
Mrs Patricia Heatley
Bevis Hillier
Mike Hodgson
Miss.S Hughes-Rowlands
Keith Hutton & Richard Morley
John Ingram
Kay Jackman, LLAM. FLAM.
Rosemary May Jackson
Gerry Jarvis
Rodney Kempster
Don Kennedy
Clifford & Eileen Knowles
Chris Lancaster
John Langford
Kit Lawie
Gary & Lorna Leach
Mr & Mrs M.R.Learwood-Griffiths
Horace Liberty
Mr Marley R. Lippiatt
The Revd. Robert LLoyd
Clyde Malby
Patricia Mann
Pat & Bernard Mattimore
Cherry Mawle

LIST OF SUBSCRIBERS

Bill Mawle
Pat McNulty (Irish musician & poet)
Ann Miller
Ben Moorhead
Baz & Sheila Morris
Clive Murphy
John & Virginia Murray
Charles J. Nancarrow
John Naylor
Miss U. A. H. Neil
James Oxley-Brennan
Hugh & Elisabeth Parkman
David Pattison
John C. Peach
Andrew C.H.(Newman) Pellow
Revd. Brian F. Peters
Jean Peters
Dr Anthony Phillips & Mrs Victoria Phillips
Bill Pickard
I.D.Gwynne Pickering
Molly & Brian Renshaw
Margaret & Martin Revill
Paul Richards
Michael Richardson
Mr Peter Dudley Roberts (retired-tired engineer/pianist)
Jean Rollason
Revd. Canon John Salter
David J. Savage
Robert Shaw
John Shearer ("Ian Douglas")
Mrs M.D.Sidey
Robert Simpson
Bernard A.J.Slatter
Mr D.F.Smith
Francis Smith
Jim Sterling
Dean Sutton
Graham Swift
John Sykes
Martin C. Tardiff
Sarah M. Taylor & Martin I. Taylor
Mrs Elizabeth Thomas
James P.S. Thomson
Mrs Nicholas Treadaway
Ann Vernau
Nigel M. Waring
Gayne Wells
John Wickens
David Anthony Williams
Stephen Willis
M.J.Wilson
Judith R. Wren
Colin Wright
Mrs Jane Edred Wright
Christopher Wyke
Mike & Wendy Yolland & Family
Tony Yolland
Michael S.Young